Thread Painting
A Garden Quilt

Thread Painting
A Garden Quilt

A Step-by-Step Guide to Creating a Realistic 6-Block Project

Joyce Hughes

Landauer Publishing

Thread Painting A Garden Quilt

Landauer Publishing, *www.landauerpub.com*, is an imprint of Fox Chapel Publishing Company, Inc.
Copyright © 2020 by Joyce Hughes and Fox Chapel Publishing Company, Inc., 903 Square Street, Mount Joy, PA 17552.

Project Team
Editor: Katie Ocasio
Copy Editor: Hayley DeBerard
Designer: Wendy Reynolds
Indexer: Nancy Arndt
Photographers: Mike Mihalo Photography (jacket and pages 2, 6, 7, 9, 29, 31, 43, 54–55, 63, 70, 71, 72, 75, 94, 95, 98, 99, 100, and 125); Joyce Hughes (step-by-step photography); Photographee.eu/Shutterstock (pages 9 and 28–29); Maryna Jack/Shutterstock (pages 10–11); and Thorsten Schmitt/Shutterstock (page 12).

Library of Congress Cataloging-in-Publication Data

Names: Hughes, Joyce, 1961- author.
Title: Thread painting a garden quilt / Joyce Hughes.
Description: Mount Joy : Landauer Publishing, [2020] | Includes index. |
 Summary: "Contains information on the supplies and techniques needed for
 creating a thread-painted Block of the Month quilt. Also includes
 step-by-step instructions and templates for completing each block"–
 Provided by publisher.
Identifiers: LCCN 2020022492 (print) | LCCN 2020022493 (ebook) | ISBN
 9781947163485 (paperback) | ISBN 9781607658184 (ebook)
Subjects: LCSH: Embroidery, Machine–Patterns. | Machine
 quilting–Patterns.
Classification: LCC TT772 .H84 2020 (print) | LCC TT772 (ebook) | DDC
 746.44028–dc23
LC record available at https://lccn.loc.gov/2020022492
LC ebook record available at https://lccn.loc.gov/2020022493

We are always looking for talented authors. To submit an idea, please send a brief inquiry to
acquisitions@foxchapelpublishing.com.

Printed in Singapore
23 22 21 20 2 4 6 8 10 9 7 5 3 1

Dedication

This book is dedicated to my Aunt Ann,
who passed away from breast cancer while I was
writing this book. I saw her love for her family
and close friends and the determination to push
through the most trying days and never give up.
She was always so proud and happy for me
during my quilting journeys and pushing me to
give my best every day. May your English garden
in Heaven be as beautiful as you.

Contents

Introduction

As a child, I always loved to color. The greatest gifts I would receive were new coloring books and a big box of crayons, so I am not surprised that I love using threads as much as I do. Sewing was a different story, however. I never enjoyed sewing as a child because I always had trouble with the machine, making a bird's nest out of my bobbin thread and breaking needles constantly. So when I started sewing many decades later, my mother was shocked and puzzled as to why I would want to start.

Soon after I learned to sew, I discovered so many different colors and types of threads. I was so excited just to play! I could see the changes on the fabric when I layered the thread colors, added metallic threads, bobbin work, and embellishments. My head would be spinning with ideas and I was hooked. Now, I can truly say I love playing with threads and I love sewing—both of which come together when creating thread-painted quilts.

When I first started to thread paint, I noticed that adding layers and layers of threads to a quilt can cause distortion, puckering, and misshaping of the quilt. On my own, I had to figure out when to layer thread and what and what not to do with the threads, fabrics, and quilting to ensure the quilt would be flat and square. Through much trial and error, I was able to achieve the desired result. I wrote this book so I could share the knowledge I gained, and you can learn the wonderful technique of thread painting without all of the headache I endured.

Tip

Thread painting is when you add pops of color and dimension to a quilt with various threads. Think of it as "painting" images onto your quilt using free-motion machine sewing.

How This Book Works

The book is laid out for the quilter to follow the detailed steps of how, when, and where to quilt and thread paint with raw-edge appliqué, adding sashing, and additional blocks to complete a flat and square quilt. Extreme attention is focused on the thread painting for adding shading, highlighting, dimension, and definition to a design element. You will build and sew each block, watching the quilt grow with each chapter into a beautiful piece of art!

One of the best ways to make a quilt pop is to add some thread painting. Thread painting is just like it sounds, "painting" with threads where the needle is your brush and the threads are your paint. The threads add color, highlights, and detail to create texture, depth, and dimension to the quilt. It is done with free-motion stitching, using several different stitches and layering multiple threads. It may look and sound complicated, but it is easier than you think. When you honor the process, you will be rewarded with an amazingly beautiful and detailed work of art.

Thread painting is a very fun, freeing, and forgiving way to sew—but saying that, there are some concerns and considerations that you need to think about: the amounts of threads added, where and when to free-motion quilt, how to prevent puckering and pleating on the fabric, keeping the blocks square, and what to do if some of these issues become a problem. To ensure a flat and square quilt, it is very important to follow the steps of this book. Desirably, you will follow the included designs and possibly add a few personal elements to create your own masterpiece!

PART I

Prepping for the Quilt

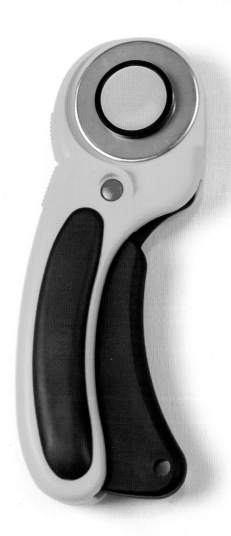

As you prepare to make your very own thread-painted quilt, it's helpful to gather your supplies, review the techniques for cutting and tracing your appliqué, and learn more about the different approaches to thread painting. Use this section as a resource as you begin working on your quilt.

CHAPTER 1

Supplies

Before you start to sew, I suggest you get organized and select the supplies needed for the quilt. I have listed suggested fabrics, threads, machines, and notions used to complete the project quilt. Some items are necessary, while others are helpful suggestions as noted.

Feel free to change the colors of the fabrics and threads as desired, keeping in mind that changes may affect the appearance of your finished quilt.

Fabrics

APPLIQUÉ PIECES

Approximately ⅛–¼ yard (11.5–23cm) batik and ombré cotton fabrics in a variety of colors. I suggest six to eight different shades of each color to help with shading and depth of design.

This quilt is a great way to use up smaller fabric pieces in your stash or all those scraps you have left over from other quilt projects. Fabrics used for the raw-edge appliqué in the project quilt are mostly batiks and ombré cotton, which allow for a lot of colors and shading from one fabric. I looked for colors that blended well together with a smooth transition to create an eye-pleasing color palette.

BACKGROUND FABRIC

2⅓ yards (2.13m) pale green cotton or batik, sub-cut into individual sizes as listed for each block (these measurements are slightly larger than the actual size used).

This appliqué was created by using scraps of fabric from my stash. They were chosen based on their colors rather than the fabric pattern or collection.

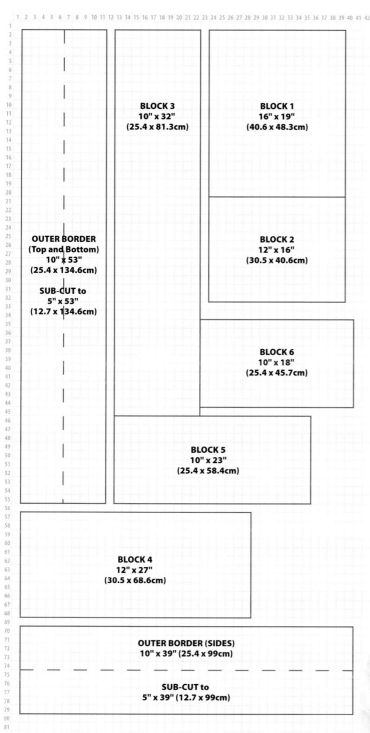

Background fabric 2⅓ yds. (2.13m)

SASHING PIECES AND FINISHED BACKING

1½ yards (1.37m) extra-wide medium blue fabric, sub-cut for backing and the individual sizes listed with each block. For finishing the backing, cut to 58" (1.5m) wide x 54" (1.4m) long (set aside for later use). Sub-cut the sashing pieces when directed for each block.

BINDING

¾ yards (0.7m) medium blue cotton fabric. Sub-cut to desired width of binding (I cut to 2½" [6.4cm]) x total size of the quilt.

STABILIZING BACKING AND BATTING

Twin size or extra-wide batting and muslin backing, cut down to 58" (1.47m) wide x 54" (1.37m) long (one whole piece of each batting and muslin backing).

I use Warm & Natural® cotton batting by The Warm Company® layered with a light-colored cotton muslin on all my projects. I layer the batting and muslin together, which acts as a stabilizer and solid foundation for the quilting and thread-painting techniques covered in this book. A stabilizer is needed to help reduce or eliminate puckering, stitch distortion, and shrinkage.

Stabilizing backing and batting

Sewing Machine and Feet

SEWING MACHINE

The quilt featured in this book was completed on a domestic sewing machine. The machine does not have to be the "newest, biggest, and best" to complete this quilt, but some features are needed and are very helpful! The features I look for are:

- Space between the needle and the machine housing on the right. A larger space gives you extra room to maneuver the fabric. An additional table extension is very helpful. When there is less bulk, drag, and pull on the fabric, a smoother stitch is created.
- The ability to do free-motion quilting with a straight and zigzag stitch. When doing free-motion quilting and thread painting, the feed dogs need to be dropped to allow the fabric to move freely under the foot.
- The option to use different feet, such as an open toe and free motion.

MACHINE FEET

Two different feet are used throughout this book, each with its own purpose:

- **Free-motion foot:** Used for free-motion quilting and thread painting.
- **Open-toe foot:** Use this foot to sew on sashing, borders, bias tape, and binding.

To thread paint, you will need to be able to change the machine feet to an open-toe foot (left) and a free-motion foot (right).

When you have ample space between the needle and the machine house, moving the fabric around as you thread paint will be much easier.

Threads

WEIGHT AND TYPE

There are so many threads in the quilting market that you can easily get confused, wondering what and when to use them. Threads differ by weight, types, plies, colors, and purpose. I will focus on the threads that I use for my quilting and thread painting.

The most important concern to me is the thread weight. Thread weights are measured by the thickness of the thread, ranging from 12 weights to 100 weights. The lower the number, the thicker the thread and vice versa. For example, 40-weight threads are thicker than 50-weight threads, 50-weight threads are thicker than 60-weight threads, etc.

The weight isn't the only consideration. I also go by appearance and the feel of the thread. Even if the labels say a specific weight, some threads look and feel thicker than others.

Another important consideration is the thread type. I prefer cotton or cotton blend for top threads and polyester for bobbin threads, but this is not a hard and fast rule. Below are some specific threads I use over and over.

- **Free-motion quilting:** I use Mettler® Poly Sheen, which is a thin thread. I use a thinner thread when I want the stitching to be less visible and not my main focus on the project (as on your thread-painted areas). Areas I free-motion quilt are the backgrounds and sashing areas.
- **Thread painting:** For top threads, I use Mettler Silk Finished Cotton 50 Multi and Poly Sheen Multi variegated colors. For the solid colors, I use Mettler Silk Finished Cotton 50, which has a nice feel and a slightly thicker appearance. The stitching shows up very well and allows for nice shading and blending of thread colors. Metallic threads create many interesting results and are wonderful for added effects, such as the shine on a leaf or watering can. For bobbin threads, I use Mettler Poly Sheen. It is a polyester thread that is stronger and thinner than cotton threads used on the top. It is best to use a thinner weight on the bottom to balance out the thread thickness and prevent your work from getting too stiff or distorted. This avoids having to adjust the machine tension.

VARIEGATED, SOLID, AND METALLIC THREADS

When thread painting, I like to use variegated, solid, and metallic thread to add depth and dimension to my designs. I've included a complete list of the thread colors I used on the project quilt, but feel free to experiment with your own combinations. For more information on choosing colors, see page 24.

I use thinner threads, such as Mettler® Poly Sheen, for free-motion quilting the background and sashing areas.

Be sure to use a top thread that will easily show up to create stunning thread-painted images.

Use a polyester thread with a thinner weight in the bobbin to balance out the thickness of the heavier cotton thread on the top.

Complete Thread List

Here is a list of the specific threads I used for the quilt in this book. If you're using a different thread brand, use the color chart at www.amann-mettler.com to compare color numbers and shades.

Top Threads

Mettler Poly Sheen
(solid colors):
- #5650 – light green to match background fabric
- #4230 – light blue to match sashing fabric

Mettler Poly Sheen Multi
(variegated colors):
- #9935 – pastels
- #9932 – greens
- #9923 – pinks
- #9924 – oranges
- #9912 – purples
- #9930 – blues

Mettler Silk Finished Cotton 50 Multi
(variegated colors):
- #9817, #9818 – greens
- #9858 – oranges
- #9852, #9855 – browns
- #9848 – reds
- #9827, #9859 – yellows
- #9838 – purples
- #9812 – blues
- #9843 – grays
- #9813 – blue/black

Mettler Silk Finished Cotton 50 (solid colors):
- #0092, #0224, #0314, #0757, #0905, #1314 – greens

- #0024, #0339, #0611, #1394, #1440 – blues
- #0122, #0163, #0790, #1074, #1334 – oranges
- #0029, #0046, #1062, #1085 – purples
- #0067, #0076, #0105, #0111, #0869, #1056, #1062, #1352, #1392, #1423 – pinks/reds
- #0120, #0608, #0899, #1412, #1533, #2263, #2522, #3507 #1392, #1423 – yellows
- #0263, #0264, #0380, #0832, #1002, #1425 – browns
- #0348, #0415, #0416 – grays
- #3000 – white
- #4000 – black

Mettler Metallic
(metallic colors):
- #5833 – green
- #2108, #1134 – golds
- #2701 – silver

Superior Threads Razzle Dazzle™ (metallic color):
- #251 – Icicle

Bobbin Threads

Mettler Poly Sheen
(solid colors):
- #5650 – green
- #4230 – blue
- #1346 – brown
- #0704 – yellow
- #2920 – purple
- #3541 – maroon
- #0015 – white
- #0020 – black

This quilt uses a true rainbow of colors. Above are some of the variegated threads I used.

Needles

Nothing is more frustrating than when your thread frays or breaks, your machine skips stitches, or your needle breaks. You can avoid these problems by choosing the appropriate needle for the specific thread you're using. When the correct combination of thread and needle is used, you will have a better stitch and more success with sewing.

- **Free-motion quilting:** I use a Schmetz Topstitch 80/12 needle for free-motion quilting. This topstitch needle has a deeper groove, which provides more protection for the thread. It also has a large eye, which is good for free-motion quilting. The 80/12 needle works well for light- to medium-stitch density, such as background quilting, skies, etc., because this needle size creates smaller holes in the fabric and is less visible. There is nothing worse than big holes throughout the background or sky. A 80/12 needle paired with Poly Sheen thread creates beautiful stitch.

- **Thread painting:** I use a Schmetz Topstitch 90/14 for thread painting. The 90/14 has a slightly thicker blade and larger eye than the 80/12,

making it a stronger needle. I increase the size to accommodate the thicker threads and the dense stitching of thread painting. The thicker threads and the motion of thread painting while blending and shading can cause extra pull on the needle, so a strong, thick needle is a bonus. The 90/14 needle works well with Mettler Silk Finished Cotton 50 thread. If your threads continue to break or fray, increase the needle size to 100/16.

I highly recommend having several packs of needles on hand when starting a new project. When you are thread painting, you will go through many layers of fabric, adhesives, and threads. The needle is penetrating through these layers and thick density, which will cause the point to get dull. A dull point causes the sewing machine to work harder to create the stitches. Often, a dull point will cause skipped stitches and broken threads. I recommend changing the needle when thread problems arise or after four to five hours of high-density stitching.

The 80/12 needle size (left) works best for free-motion quilting, and the thicker 90/14 needle size (right) works best for thread painting.

Other Necessary Supplies

LITE STEAM-A-SEAM 2® OR HOTFIX ADHESIVE™ (APPROXIMATELY 6 YARDS [5.5M])

When ironed onto the wrong side of the fabric, these products adhere two materials together, holding the appliqué and background fabrics together (follow the instructions included with the product on how to apply).

Lite Steam-A-Seam 2 is repositionable until ironed in place. It is also lightweight, which is best for a sewable bond and helps fabrics keep their soft feel.

Often used for mechanically cutting fabric, Hotfix Adhesive is slightly stiffer and easier to feed into the machine after ironing. This allows for nice, clean cuts, but when the backing is removed, the fabric is very soft and can be stitched over with no issues.

LIGHT BOX/BOARD

You will need to trace the patterns onto freezer paper or regular printer paper (when using a cutting machine). I suggest using a light box/board. I use CutterPillar™ Glow Premium light board. This light board has a nonglare adjustable bright LED lighting, which is helpful to see the detailed patterns. This specific light board also has a tempered glass-cutting mat. The bonus of the glass mat is you can cut and iron directly on it. I use the glass mat (similar to the pressing cloth) when joining multiply pieces together to create one design.

PENCILS AND PAPER

Use a sharp pencil to trace the patterns onto freezer paper or printer paper. Trace the designs onto freezer paper, then iron them onto your fabric (page 21). Freezer paper is reusable, so if you need to make more than one item such as leaves, you can re-iron the freezer paper onto the fabric several times. You do not need to retrace the leaves multiple times.

If you're using a cutting machine, trace your patterns onto printer paper instead (see page 22).

PRESSING CLOTH

Pressing cloths can be very helpful when building appliqué pieces. I place the numerous pieces of a single design on top of the pressing cloth, then iron the pieces together to make one whole piece. The pressing cloth allows the intended pieces to bond

Light board

Pressing cloth

together while protecting your work surface from the adhesive.

IRON (LARGE AND SMALL) AND A WOOL MAT

I recommend you have both small and large steam irons on hand that are capable of getting very hot. Use the irons on freezer paper, fabrics, Lite Steam-N-Seam 2, Hotfix Adhesive, bias tape, and crystals. The small iron is helpful when ironing small appliqué pieces together. Use a wool mat whenever you need to iron your thread painting: it will prevent the threads from being crushed and will preserve their raised texture.

HOT-FIXED CRYSTALS

Iron-on crystals have a heat-activated adhesive on the back side that will adhere to the fabric when ironed in place. Add these to draw attention to specific areas of the quilt.

Rotary cutter and small scissors

Fabric-safe marking pens

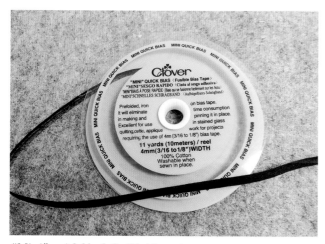

"Mini" quick black fusible bias tape

ROTARY CUTTER AND SMALL SCISSORS

A rotary cutter is helpful when cutting large straight blocks, sashing, borders, and binding. Small, sharp scissors are useful when cutting the appliqué pieces and snipping threads very close to the fabric.

FABRIC-SAFE MARKING PENS

There are plenty of marking tools on the market, but I like to use water-soluble pens and chalk. Before you use any marking tool on your project, test on a piece of scrap; colors are harder to remove and can leave a residue. Use pens or chalk to square a quilt and mark free-motion quilting designs.

ASSORTMENT OF LARGE RULERS AND TAPE MEASURE

When marking and squaring a quilt, I use the largest ruler possible. My favorites are Omnigrid's® Omnigrip® rulers in sizes 20.5" x 20.5" (0.5 x 0.5m) and 8" x 24" (20.3 x 61cm). They allow you to check several lines (vertical and horizontal) on the quilt at the same time. More reference lines allow you to square the blocks and sashing perfectly!

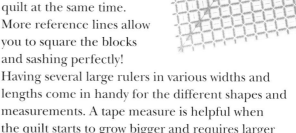

Having several large rulers in various widths and lengths come in handy for the different shapes and measurements. A tape measure is helpful when the quilt starts to grow bigger and requires larger measurements for cutting and squaring the quilt.

"MINI" QUICK BLACK FUSIBLE BIAS TAPE

Use bias tape in the final steps to square the blocks with a solid black outline. The tape has a layer of adhesive on the back side, which is ironed in place then sewn.

SAFETY PINS AND STRAIGHT PINS

Use safety pins to pin the top, batting, and backing together before free motion quilting the layers. Straight pins are for pinning straight edges together before you sew.

Helpful Optional Supplies

ELECTRONIC CUTTING MACHINE

I like to use the Brother® ScanNCut. This machine allows you to scan the designs directly into the machine, then the prepared fabric is fed into the machine to cut out the individual pieces.

For this book, I recommend photocopying the designs to be used with your machine. Some pieces may be very small, however, and it might be best to hand-cut these pieces.

CLEAR PLASTIC SANDWICH BAGS

Clear bags are very useful for holding all your prepped adhesive fabrics. I keep all similarly colored fabrics in individual bags. As an example, when I need brown, I can look at the bag of brown fabrics and possibly use these for what I need for completing the next designs.

FABRIC PENCILS

Use fabric pencils to add shading to the fabric and mark the direction of thread paint. I like to use high-quality, artist-grade colored pencils, such as Prismacolor Premier® brand.

BIKE CLAMPS

Bike clamps are helpful to use when quilting and thread painting a large piece. Roll up the quilt and attach the clamps to keep the quilt together and prevent the weight of the quilt from pulling and creating drag. This will keep the weight balanced as you sew.

LARGE FOAM BOARD

A large foam board (purchased at a hardware store) works well as a design board but is also very helpful when attaching the backing to the quilt. I pin the backing to the foam board, then pin together the quilt to the backing prior to quilting.

Brother® ScanNCut

Fabric pencils

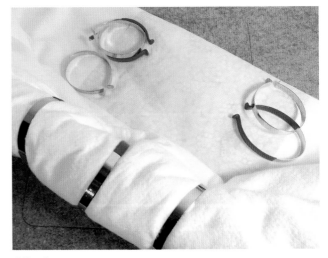

Bike clamps

CHAPTER 2

Tracing and Cutting Designs

Before you start thread painting your blocks, you need to assemble and fuse the appliqué pieces to your background fabric. In this chapter I will go over my preferred methods for applying fusible adhesive to your fabrics, tracing the appliqué templates, and cutting out your shapes.

Applying Adhesive to Fabrics

Raw-edge appliqué requires that you apply an adhesive to your fabrics before cutting out the shapes.

I use Lite Steam-A-Seam 2® by the Warm Company for my appliqué fabrics. Lite Steam-A-Seam 2 is a lightweight double-stick fusible web. When the backing is removed, the web is tacky and repositionable for the placement of the appliqué pieces, allowing you to redesign your block as desired. Follow the manufacturer's directions for adhering the fusible to the wrong side of your fabric.

Prep all your fabrics for a block at once, and use clear plastic bags to keep your colors organized. For example, if your block calls for four greens, prep all four shades and store them in the same bag. As you continue to work on your quilt and build new blocks, you can reuse these fabrics, especially when you only need small amounts.

Tracing, Cutting Out, and Ironing Patterns

Once you have prepped your fabrics, it's time to work on the templates. If you're using scissors to cut out your pieces, make sure you have a sharp pencil and freezer paper ready to go.

1. With a sharp pencil, trace the designs with the identifying number for each piece onto the *dull* side of the freezer paper. Use a light box if you have one.

Use the designs in this book as inspiration. Don't feel like your block designs have to look identical to mine!

If a design has multiple parts, assemble them after completing all five steps to create one piece. Remember to use a pressing cloth or tempered-glass mat under the fabric when you iron the parts together.

2. Cut all the individual designs from the freezer paper, leaving ¼" (0.6cm) around each design. If a design consists of multiple parts, keep all those pieces together.

3. With a hot iron, press the freezer paper pieces onto the right side of the fabric. For pieces marked 'R' (reverse), press the pattern piece onto the wrong side of the fabric.

4. With sharp scissors, cut out all the pieces along the lines. You'll be cutting through freezer paper, fabric, and adhesive web. Leave the freezer paper on the fabric until using the piece—this will help to keep all the pieces together when you assemble the design.

5. Remove the paper backing from the fusible adhesive. The back of the fabric pieces should be tacky. Iron the pieces in place, following the directions for your specific block.

Arrange the blocks as *suggested* on the pattern. If your pieces are slightly smaller or bigger, that is okay! Some pieces may need tucking under or over the different parts. This is not an exact placement pattern. Play around with the placement until you are happy with the layout. When you like the arrangement, place the pressing cloth on top and iron in place. The iron will heat the glue, creating a permanent bond of appliqué pieces to background fabric.

Cutting with a Mechanical Cutter

If you're using a mechanical cutter, follow the manufacturer's instructions for your specific machine.

I use Hotfix Adhesive™ on the fabrics that I cut using a mechanical cutter such as Brother ScanNCut. This product does not have the same tacky feel of Lite Steam-N-Seam 2, but it will feed through the machine. Apply Hotfix Adhesive to the back of the fabric then cut into 8" x 12" (20.3 x 30.5cm) sheets (same size of pattern pages) or smaller, and feed evenly into the machine to cut.

To cut the fabric pieces out, you may need to scan and copy the appliqué templates in the back of this book. Once cut, you can arrange your pieces and iron them onto your background fabric.

Cutting machines, like the Brother ScanNCut shown here, will help you save time when there are many small pieces to cut.

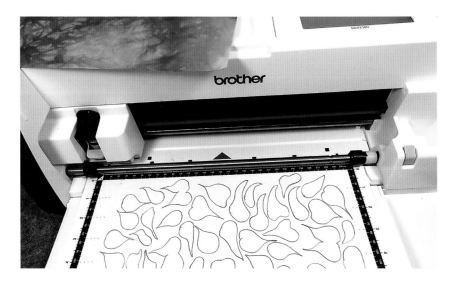

CHAPTER 3

Thread-Painting Basics

It's almost time to start making the quilt, but first let's review the basic stitching techniques you'll use in each block. You'll find detailed directions for thread painting in each element of your quilt in the specific block instructions, but it's helpful to have a general understanding of the process first.

Free-Motion Quilting

You'll notice in the quilt instructions that you will quilt each assembled block before adding the thread-painted details. By quilting the background first, you add stability to your block, and there will be less distortion and puckering along the edges of your appliqué designs.

There are many wonderful resources devoted entirely to free-motion quilting, but for our purposes, we will stick to the basics. If you haven't tried free-motion quilting before, practice on some scrap fabric before moving onto your quilt.

Tip

It's important to take breaks when you're free-motion quilting to rest your brain and muscles. When you pause to rest or reposition your fabric, choose a spot that won't be very noticeable.

SET UP YOUR MACHINE

Before you sit down to quilt, clean your sewing area, and get rid of clutter. You need room around your sewing machine to move the quilt freely.

Drop the feed dogs on your machine. You'll be using your hands to guide the quilt.

Make sure you're using a free-motion foot—you need to be able to see your needle as you're quilting.

Check the needle in your machine. I recommend a topstitch 80 needle for free-motion quilting. Thread your machine with a lightweight thread, such as Mettler Poly Sheen.

SECURE YOUR THREAD

You're ready to start quilting. The first thing you need to do is secure your thread. Follow these steps:

1. Start with the needle in the down position.

2. Take one stitch in place, then stop to pull up the bobbin thread.

3. Take two or three stitches backward and sew over the first stitch. This will secure your thread.

4. Clip your thread tails and continue quilting.

TIPS FOR FREE-MOTION QUILTING

As I mentioned before, practice your free-motion quilting on scrap fabric before you move onto your quilt. Getting the speed of your machine just right, feeling comfortable with the pressure on your foot pedal, and understanding how to move the fabric takes practice. The goal is to create nice, evenly spaced stitches. If you move the fabric too quickly, you may get big, open stitches, and if you move too slowly, your stitches will be tiny.

Choose an open, flowing design for your background. If your stitches are too close and tight, the quilt will become distorted and stiff. Designs without noticeable repeats will camouflage mistakes and allow you to add in additional quilting, if needed.

When you're quilting the backgrounds on your final blocks, start along the edge of your appliqué

Correct and incorrect quilting techniques: (top left) correct amount of quilting; (top right) because there is no quilting done before thread painting, notice the puckering around the edges of the flower design; (bottom right) this block wasn't quilted to the edge of the design, which makes a bubble along edges of the flowers; (bottom left) the quilting is sloppy and too tight, creating stiffness and shrinkage of the background.

On large open areas (such as an open background), start free motion quilting along the edges of the design nearest the center of your design and do the quilting from the center out to the sides.

design, somewhere near the center. You'll work from the center out to the sides, overlapping about two to three stitches into the design. This overlap will later get covered with your thread painting, and will help prevent a bubble from forming between the design and your background.

Beginning to Thread Paint

CHOOSING COLORS

Although I've included the specific threads used on each block of the quilt so that you can re-create your blocks as close to mine as you'd like, it's helpful to understand how and why I chose the colors I did, in case you'd like to experiment with your own threads.

When picking top threads for thread painting, I use the colors of the fabric as a guide. This helps to match the correct color tone and value. With thread painting, you want the colors to blend into the work rather than contrast with your fabric.

Bobbin threads should be within the same color family as the top thread. If you do see the bottom thread on top, it will eventually be covered with additional threads and blended in.

The first threads selected for a project are variegated. I use variegated threads as my "base" in blending. When choosing a variegated thread, notice if there are different shades of one color or multiple colors. I tend to choose the variegated threads with several shades of one color. When working on nature and landscape projects, the blending of shades from a single color looks more natural. If there are several different colors in the variegation, chances are the colors will stitch out in the wrong places.

When choosing the variegated threads, place the threads over the area to be stitched. Be cautious of threads being too extreme in color value. You do not want very light-colored threads stitched on dark fabric and vice versa. Look for a mixed blend between the fabric and variegated threads, blending the lights and darks together.

For added depth to an area, choose two different variegated threads. See the image on the facing page for an example. In the area where several leaves meet, I stitched some leaves with one variegated green thread and the remaining leaves with a different variegated green thread. Often, areas stitched out with all the same threads look flat.

After choosing and stitching the variegated threads, select the solid threads, in both solid cotton and a shiny metallic. Look for solid-colored threads from the variegated thread colors. I typically use solid colors to shade, highlight, and define a design. Working with at least two to five colors in a color family helps to achieve the proper effects of thread

The base of this plant is stitched with two variegated thread spools in varying shades of green that closely match the color of the leaves. This gives the leaves of the plant more depth.

Choose the solid cotton and metallic threads based on the variegated thread colors.

painting. The additional threads create a smooth and gradual blend of colors.

To select the solid colors, place the solid threads onto the area sewn with the variegated threads. Pick the lightest solid color from the medium variegated color. The next solid color is a shade or two darker, and so on until you pick all of the solid colors. If the solid colors blend into the variegated threads and fabric, choose one shade darker, and add additional threads. You will almost always want to go darker rather than lighter.

Thread-Painting Cheat Sheet

If you need a quick refresher of the basic steps, use this list:

- Make sure to drop your feed dogs and your free-motion foot is on your machine.
- Use a Schmetz Topstitch 90/14 or similar needle.
- Match the bobbin thread (lighter weight) to the color family of the top thread.
- Start with zigzag stitches:

  - Use variegated threads, such as Mettler Variegated Silk Finished 50 and Poly Sheen Multi. Base thread colors on the colors of the appliqué pieces.
  - Change your machine settings to width 2.0 and length 0.0 (or lowest length machine will go). For small designs, decrease stitch width to 1.5.
  - Work around your appliqué pieces, stitching on all edges of the design. Then add some stitching inside the design to blend and add shading.
- Switch to straight stitches:
  - Do NOT change stitch width or length.
  - Work straight stitches with solid threads such as Mettler Silk Finished Solid 50 and metallic threads.
  - Choose 2–5 solid colors based on the colors in the variegated thread you're layering over.
  - Start with the lightest of your solid threads and work to the darkest. If you have a metallic, add that in before the darkest thread.

The metallic thread color should blend in with the solid colors, but add a fun and subtly sparkly highlight. Using a metallic thread is one of the best ways to really make your entire thread painting stand out. I like to see how the different colors blend to create amazing effects. Remember, if you're going to all the trouble to layer in these colors, you want to see your work!

When all the quilting and thread painting on the block/blocks is finished, the quilt will need to be ironed flat before moving on to squaring the blocks to build to the next step. You may find bumps or bubbles in areas with uneven quilting or thread painting. To fix this, simply add some stitching over the bubble. Add whimsical curlicues, branches, grass, or simply free-motion quilt over it. However, if you add a curlicue, add some more elsewhere in the block/quilt so it looks balanced, but do NOT add the curlicues until instructed to do so.

STITCHING THE LAYERS

Again, the instructions for this quilt will walk you through the specific process for thread painting each of these blocks, but let's go over the basic process first.

The blocks in this quilt are stitched one at a time for a reason: because of the multiple layers of stitching you're adding to your quilt, the blocks can get very dense and distorted. Working on small areas of the quilt at a time helps minimize puckering. Complete a section of the quilt before starting the next—don't bounce around the quilt.

BASE STITCHING

Your first layer of stitching, called the base layer, is done with a zigzag stitch. It's important to understand that the stitch you're creating will not look like a true "zigzag." Once you've adjusted your machine settings, place the area to be sewn under the needle, and move the fabric side to side, left to right. When you move the fabric this way, you'll create a serrated line that looks almost like a straight stitch. The stitch length should not be uniform.

If you do start to see a true zigzag stitch form, pause with your needle in the down position, and pivot the fabric, so you can continue sewing side to side. Remember to pivot the fabric as the direction of your design changes.

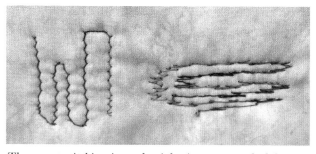

The correct stitching is on the right; incorrect on the left.

Zigzag stitching is the first part of the thread-painting process. Stitch all the edges of the design and also inside to blend and add shading.

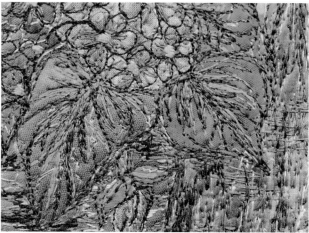

Here are some samples of other leaves I've done for the book's project.

This cluster of leaves alternates threads to create depth and dimension.

Here is a sample of appliqué sunflowers to show the detailing of the stitching. Note in the sample that both flowers have the same yellow and brown fabric. The difference is the color of threads used. See how the different colors and layering of threads affect the look of the flower? The numbers written on the fabric indicate the amount of solid-colored threads used in that area.

The goal of this zigzag layer is to help anchor and stabilize your fabric. You'll add more detail in the following layers.

ADDITIONAL STITCHING

After your base of zigzag stitches is complete, you'll add in multiple layers of straight stitching to add detail and depth to your designs. A small, irregular stitch length (which you can create with rocking back-and-forth motion) will help your colors blend and add natural shading.

Start with the lightest of your thread colors, and end with the darkest. If you're working on a cluster of the same design (for example, you have many a group of three leaves), alternate the thread colors so that the thread painting within the leaves is not identical. Use all four colors in one leaf, and use different combinations of three colors in the remaining leaves.

If you're using metallic thread, add it before the final and darkest thread layer. Metallic threads can be difficult to sew with, so slow down your speed and use a thread stand. The stand will help the thread relax and unwind prior to going through the tension disc.

Complete several layers within a single design (flower, leaf, etc.) at a time for shading, highlighting, and final detail stitching. Pay attention to the direction of your stitching, and follow the contours of the appliqué piece.

Do not try to avoid or purposely sew on the variegated threads. Add these solid-colored threads to blend and add to the thread work.

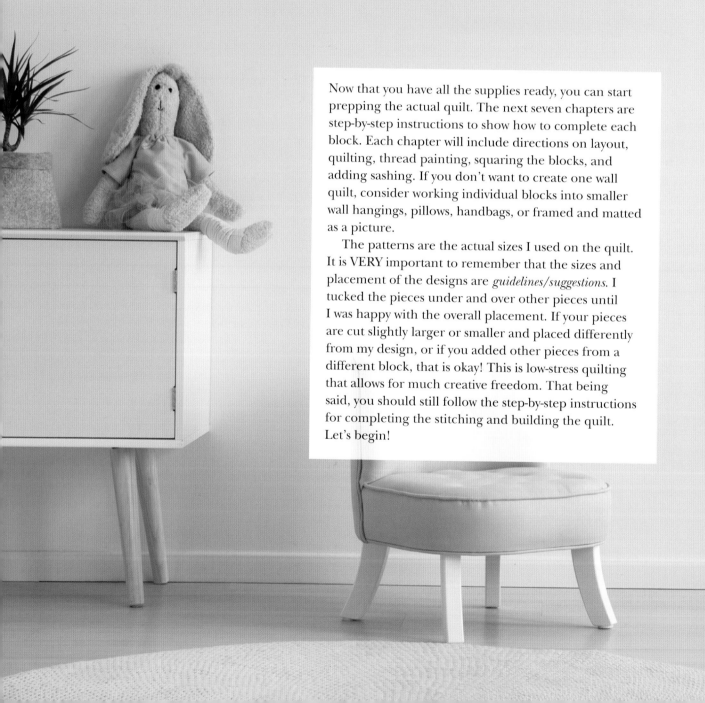

PART II

The Quilt Project

Now that you have all the supplies ready, you can start prepping the actual quilt. The next seven chapters are step-by-step instructions to show how to complete each block. Each chapter will include directions on layout, quilting, thread painting, squaring the blocks, and adding sashing. If you don't want to create one wall quilt, consider working individual blocks into smaller wall hangings, pillows, handbags, or framed and matted as a picture.

The patterns are the actual sizes I used on the quilt. It is VERY important to remember that the sizes and placement of the designs are *guidelines/suggestions*. I tucked the pieces under and over other pieces until I was happy with the overall placement. If your pieces are cut slightly larger or smaller and placed differently from my design, or if you added other pieces from a different block, that is okay! This is low-stress quilting that allows for much creative freedom. That being said, you should still follow the step-by-step instructions for completing the stitching and building the quilt. Let's begin!

CHAPTER 4

Mending the Garden

Block 1

MATERIALS

- ✛ Pattern, page 101
- ✛ Batting: Warm & Natural Batting and Muslin, cut to 58" (1.47m) wide x 54" (1.37m) length and ironed flat (Each individual item will need to be a single piece, not pieced to get these measurements. If the batting or muslin is pieced, you may possibly have seams showing through the top.)
- ✛ Background: light green batik, cut to 19" x 15½" (48.3 x 39.4cm)
- ✛ Freezer paper
- ✛ Appliqué fabric suggestions: batiks and ombré cottons in medium gray, dark gray, medium blue, medium brown, dark brown, tan, yellow, black, pink, and variety of purples and greens

- **Watering can:** medium gray (#1 and #3) and dark gray (#2, #4, #5, #6, and #7)
- **Shovel and trowel:** medium gray (#8 and #10) and medium blue (#9 and #11)
- **Gloves:** tan (#12 and #13) and medium blue (#14 and #15)
- **Basket:** medium brown (#16) and dark brown (#17 and #18)
- **Bird:** yellow (#19) and black (#20–23)
- **Trellis:** tan (#59–69)

- **Lavender**
Flowers: mixed medium to dark purples (#24–#29); make cluster with approx. 14–16 flowers
Stems and leaves: mixed medium to dark greens (#30–#35); make 6 stems and 6–8 leaves
- **Clematis**
Flowers and buds: medium pink (#40–#56) and yellow (#57 and #58); make approx. 7–8 flowers and 15–16 buds
Leaves: mixed light to medium greens (#36–#38); make 80–85 (save leftovers for future blocks)

THREADS

- ✛ Background: Mettler Poly sheen (match the color of the fabric)
- ✛ Variegated threads:
- • Mettler Silk Finished Cotton 50 Multi
  - #9859 – mixed tans
  - #9817 – mixed lime greens
  - #9827 – mixed yellows
  - #9838 – mixed purples
  - #9818 – mixed greens
  - #9813 – mixed dark blue and black
  - #9843 – mixed grays
  - #9855 – mixed tans

- • Mettler Poly Sheen Multi
  - #9932 – mixed greens
  - #9924 – mixed pinks
  - #9912 – mixed purples
  - #9930 – mixed blues
- ✛ Solid-colored threads:
- • Mettler Silk Finished Cotton 50
  - #0757 – dark green
  - #1314 – medium green
  - #0092 – medium green
  - #0314 – dark green
  - #1352 – dark pink
  - #0869 – maroon
  - #2263 – yellow
  - #0608 – mustard yellow
  - #1425 – brown

- #1002 – dark brown
- #1062 – medium purple
- #1085 – medium purple
- #0046 – dark purple
- #0416 – medium gray
- #0348 – dark gray
- #1425 – tan
- #0024 – teal blue
- #4000 – black
- #3000 – white
- #0899 – dark mustard yellow
- ✛ Metallic threads:
- • Mettler
  - #5833 – green
  - #2108 – gold
  - #2701 – silver

Tip
There are numbers next to the colors listed for each appliqué piece in every materials list in this book. These number correspond to the numbers displayed on each block's pattern.

Prepping and Designing

1. Layer the batting and muslin together evenly, making sure they are flat with no bumps or creases. It may be helpful to pin-baste the two layers together to keep them flat while you sew the quilt.

2. Follow the instructions for tracing and cutting on page 21.

3. After cutting out all pieces, arrange and form the individual elements (such as the clematis, trellis, gloves, lavender, bird, etc.) before making the actual layout.

Look at the pattern for suggestions and arrange the block as shown. Remember to tuck the pieces over and under each other to create a natural appearance.

> *Tip*
>
> Remove the paper backing from your pieces before you start arranging and pressing them into place.

Center and balance the design. Try not to place pieces close to the sides. Keep in mind that you will need ¼" (0.6cm) on all four sides for adding the sashing.

4. When pleased with the arrangement, place a pressing cloth on top of the block. With a hot iron, press the appliqué piece in place, adhering the pieces to the background fabric.

> *Tip*
>
> There's no pattern piece for the dark green fabric under the trellis. Rough cut a piece of fabric to approximately 4½" x 2½" (11.5 x 6.5cm) and layer it in.

Here is what the arrangement should look like before you press the appliqué pieces in place.

A close-up of the clematis and trellis.

5. Find the centers of the layered batting and muslin and Block 1. Place the block on top of the batting and pin in place. Check for even placement, measuring the exposed batting on all four sides.

A close-up of the lavender, basket, and yellow bird.

6. Free motion quilt the background following the instructions on page 23. Start from the middle and ALWAYS move from the center to the outer edges. When you are finished quilting to the edge in one section, cut the threads and start from the middle again, working your way out. Continue to free motion quilt the background until completely finished.

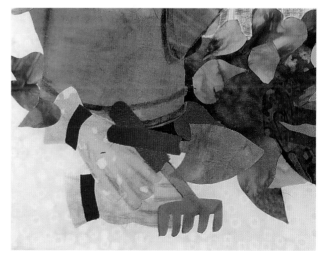

A close-up of the gardening tools.

Thread Painting

Leaving your feed dogs down, and your free-motion foot on, switch the needle on your machine to a Topstitch 90/14 needle.

The beginning of the stitching, mostly, is from the background pieces to the foreground pieces. This allows you to travel with the stitching and then cover those threads when using the next threads.

BASE STITCHING

Set up your machine for a zigzag stitch with a width of 2.0 and length of 0.0 (if the pieces are small, decrease the width to 1.5). Be mindful to sew horizontally on the piece, creating a serrated stitch (not a true zigzag or straight stitch). For the stitch design, follow the

Remember!

Quilt into a design, rather than leaving a space around the appliqué pieces.

Here you can see the whole block with all the base stitching completed.

direction of the items. For example, follow the way the petals and leaves are formed, the lines of the trellis, the direction of the feathers on the bird, etc.

1. **Trellis.** Using variegated tans, start from the center and move up and out to the sides, stitching all the small areas of the trellis. You can travel around the areas either (1) by sewing on the edge of pieces (flowers or leaves) that you know will be covered with other threads, or (2) you can jump stitch and trim those threads later.

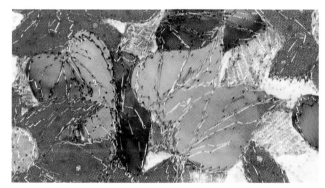

2. **Leaves.** Use two different variegated greens to create added depth and prevent the leaves from looking the same. Only use one variegated green thread per leaf. Stitch along the edges of the leaf, then create a center line and side veins.

Remember!

Change the bobbin thread to match the color family of the thread on top.

3. **Clematis flower and buds.** Use variegated pinks on the pink areas and variegated yellows on the centers. On the petals, stitch along the edges and inside the petal to add color. In the center, with circular stitching, sew along the edges and inside the middle.

4. **Basket.** Use variegated browns on the basket and handle, stitching in the direction of the handle, top band, and basket slates.

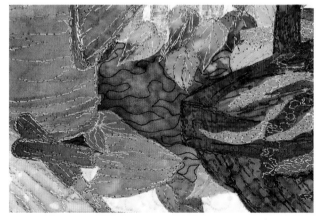

5. **Grass area.** Free motion quilt the grass with dark green solid threads. Flatten the area with some quilting, but not compete with the thread-painted appliquéd pieces.

6. Lavender flowers, leaves, and stems. Decrease the zigzag width to 1.5. Use two variegated purples on the flowers and variegated greens on the leaves and stems. The flowers are sewn with small circles, filling in the area. Only use one variegated purple thread per flower. Use variegated dark greens on the leaves and stems. Sew on the edges and add detail within the center on the leaves and stems.

7. Bird. With your stitch width still at 1.5, use the variegated yellow threads on the yellow areas and mixed dark variegated thread on the black areas. Stitch in the direction of the feathers and sew on all the outer edges of all the pieces.

8. Watering can and gardening tools. Use variegated grays on the watering can and tools and variegated blues on the tool handles. Stitch in the direction of the multiple parts, catching all the edges and adding some additional stitching in the middle of the pieces. The watering can is a large piece, so make sure to stitch in the center to flatten the piece and not create a bubble.

9. Gloves. Use variegated tans on the glove and variegated blues on the bands. Stitch on the outer edges and remember to add some lines to identify the fingers of the gloves. Remember to follow the direction of the different parts.

ADDITIONAL STITCHING

Before you start adding your solid threads, iron your quilt block to get rid of any puckers.

For the following steps, use a straight stitch and solid-colored threads. For more details, see page 27.

1. Trellis. Use a medium brown to add the detail and shading of the wood. Create a wood grain in the correct direction. Also, outline the trellis to define the edges.

2. Leaves. Use five different greens to achieve the correct shading, highlighting, definition, and depth. I used two medium greens, a metallic green, and two dark greens.

Start by adding the two medium greens randomly, and not on every leaf (only use one medium shade

This is the complete thread-painted Block 1.

per leaf). This creates depth and helps to ensure that not all the leaves look the same. Add to the outer ends and center veins to enhance the shading and highlighting of the leaf, following the decorative patterns of the leaves.

Add metallic green to create a sparkle and additional interest in the quilt.

Finish by adding dark green details and soft, blended outline along the edges. Only use one dark green per leaf.

3. Clematis flowers and buds. Start with pink thread, slightly darker than the fabric for the petals.

Next, use a slightly dark pink or maroon to blend all the colors together. Maroon is also used to outline and define the individual petals.

Tip

Be mindful of where you place your stitching. In this close-up, you can see how the pink fabric still shows through and that the thread is used only to add highlights, definition, and shading.

Layer the threads from the top with the lightest yellow and overlapping in the middle with a slightly darker yellow to create the spiky and ombré appearance of the flower centers. Finish at the bottom with metallic gold spikes.

4. Basket. Create the shading and highlighting on the basket handle and bands with a medium brown thread. You may want to go a little heavier with the threading to help shade and shape the individual bands on the basket.

Add dark brown last to define the shape and parts of the basket. Add additional markings on the basket to give it more texture and character.

5. Lavender flowers, leaves, and stems. The threads for the purple flowers are treated the same way as the clematis leaves. Start with two medium purples to shade and shape the small individual petals of the flowers.

On each flower, starting from the top and working in rows, create several half-moon shapes (while adding additional shading). Create these shapes from the top, working down to the bottom of each flower.

Mimic the same stitching as before (with the first two medium purples) but use a dark purple thread on random flowers. This will define the shapes of each individual petal.

With the medium green, highlight the edges of the leaves and stems. This will help create some separation of the leaves and stems bunched together. Use the dark green to define each leaf and stem.

instance, I sewed a little more heavily on the sides of the watering can to help create the roundness.

Next, work in metallic silver thread. Again, mimic the above stitching, but be mindful not to add too much sparkle.

Add the dark gray last, and use it sparingly, adding it only where you still need the extra definition on the pieces.

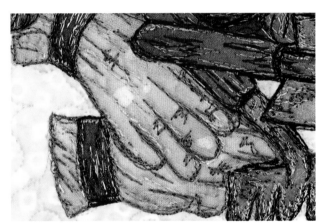

7. Gloves. Use a single tan thread, a shade darker than the fabric. Stitch along the outline of the pieces, then add in additional details where needed.

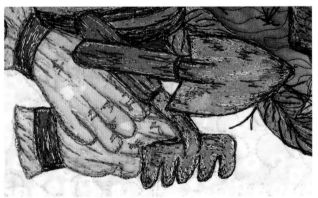

6. Watering can and tools. First start with the medium gray thread to define the individual shapes. Add the thread a little heavier where you need some separation of parts and to create some shape. For

8. Tool handles and glove bands. Use a blue thread a shade darker than your fabric, and outline the pieces. Go back in to add some shading, which also helps illustrate the direction of the pieces.

Tip

Make sure to use small stitches to give your bird a feathery texture.

9. Bird. Many layers of small stitches sewn in rows create a soft blending and shading for the appearance of feathers on the bird. Start from the tail and work up the body to the head. You may want to overlap the stitching but be mindful of the direction of the different body parts.

Using medium yellow thread, start from the tail and make your way to the head. Sew small stitches to imitate the layering of feathers.

Add mustard thread to define the bird's beak and to shade and separate the chest, wings, and neck areas.

Add black thread to the cap, wings, and tail, blending the layers of stitching into the different black and yellow areas.

Add white thread to the wings and tail, sewing in short irregular lengths to imitate the white striping. Add the bird's feet to make him appear that he's perched on the basket handle.

10. Press. Even if you have been using your iron on the block throughout the previous steps, press the block again!

11. Grass spikes or curlicues. Look for any raised bumps or uneven threading or quilting. If there are any areas of concern, try adding additional quilting or grass spikes or curlicues.

First, add the curlicues where needed, then add more throughout the piece to balance the extra stitching. Even if your block is perfectly flat, consider adding curlicues to soften the design and give the block a natural look.

Blocking and Squaring

After completing all the quilting and thread painting, the block may look misshapen. Adding Block 2 and squaring up Block 1 will help correct this issue.

BLOCKING

Before beginning, make sure the entire block is flat and able to get wet from the steam of the iron.

1. On the back side, iron the quilt/block with a very hot steam iron starting in the center and moving out to each side. Press up and out to the corners. Repeat on the bottom of the block, pressing from the center and out to the bottom corners.

2. While the quilt is face down, iron the muslin and batting area where Block 2 will be placed. Iron the layers flat, pushing out to the sides. Pinning in place is helpful. Make sure there are no bumps or pleats.

3. Flip the quilt over and repeat the ironing process. Pay extra attention to design elements that need to remain straight, such as the trellis and basket handle. If they are misshapen, pull and tug on the fabric to correct the shape. If needed, use a ruler to check the straightness of the lines. Let the quilt lie flat until it is completely dry.

SQUARING

Once completely dry, the quilt can be squared and prepared to add the right-side sashing and Block 2.

1. Place the largest ruler on Block 1 and work off as many horizontal and vertical lines on the block as possible (trellis lines, basket handle, and watering can lines). Use these as reference lines to aide in squaring the block.

2. Mark the squaring guides and connect the lines on the sides, top, and bottom. Make sure that all batting will be covered when adding the sashing. Keep in mind, the design should be centered with equal measurements on all sides, such as 2" (5cm) of background fabric on the left and right sides of block. Notice how distorted the block became from all the stitching.

3. Square the block to 18¼" x 14¾" (46.4 x 37.5cm). (If your measurements are not the same as mine, that is okay. You will make adjustments as needed.) From the marked lines, measure the width and length of the block in several places to make sure the measurements are all the same. Make sure these lines are straight because you are going to start expanding the quilt one block at a time off of these and future square lines.

It's important to be meticulous when squaring the block since it is the foundation for the rest of your quilt. The marked lines are the placement lines for adding the future sashing and blocks.

CHAPTER 5

Spring Colors

Block 2

MATERIALS

- ✢ Pattern, page 106
- ✢ Background: light green batik, cut to 11½" x 15½" (29.2 x 39.4cm)
- ✢ Sashing: light blue batik, cut to 2" x 15½" (5 x 39.4cm)
- ✢ Freezer paper
- ✢ Appliqué fabric suggestions: batiks, ombré cottons, in light brown/rust, light purple, medium purple, 4 shades of green, white, yellow, mustard yellow, dark brown, 3–4 medium pinks, white, blue, and black
- • **Pots:** light brown/rust (#1 and #2)

- • **Violets:** medium green (#3–5) and 2 different purples (#6 and #7); make approximately 8 leaves and 6 mixed purple flowers
- • **Lily of the valley:** medium green (#10–13), dark green (#14 and #15) and white (#16, #17, and #18); make total of 4 stems and 16 white flowers
- • **Grass spike fillers:** mixed greens (#19–21); make approximately 8
- • **Iris and bud:** dark green (#22–25), yellow (#27–31), purple (#26, #32, #33, and #34), mustard yellow (#35 and #36)

- • **Magnolia**
  Flowers and buds: mixed medium pinks (#40–47); make 2 flowers and 4 buds
  Bark: dark brown (#37–39); make extra as needed to connect branches
- • **Lily and bud:** white (#48–51 and #53–58), medium green (#52), yellow/pink (#53a–58a), light and medium green (#59 and #60); make approximately 6–8 leaves
- • **Butterfly:** black (#61, #62, and #63), blue (#64 and #65)

THREADS

- ✢ Background: Mettler Poly Sheen (match the color of the fabric)
- ✢ Variegated threads:
- • Mettler Silk Finished Cotton 50 Multi
  - #9852 – mixed dark browns
  - #9855 – mixed medium browns
  - #9818 – mixed greens
  - #9817 – mixed lime greens
  - #9859 – mixed yellows
  - #9838 – mixed purples
  - #9813 – mixed blue and black
- • Mettler Poly Sheen Multi
  - #9932 – mixed greens
  - #9923 – mixed pinks
  - #9935 – mixed pastels
  - #9912 – mixed light purples
  - #9930 – mixed blue

- ✢ Solid-colored threads
- • Mettler Silk Finished Cotton 50
  - #1002 – dark brown
  - #0832 – medium brown
  - #0264 – dark brown
  - #1425 – medium brown
  - #0263 – dark brown
  - #0092 – medium green
  - #0314 – dark green
  - #0314 – medium green
  - #0757 – dark green
  - #0224 – medium green
  - #0905 – dark green
  - #4000 – black
  - #1392 – pink
  - #0869 – maroon
  - #1085 – medium purple
  - #0046 – dark purple

  - #0608 – dark yellow
  - #1440 – teal blue
  - #1062 – dark purple/magenta
  - #0029 – medium purple
  - #2263 – yellow
  - #1412 – pale yellow
  - #3000 – white
  - #1056 – pale pink
  - #1423 – bright pink
  - #1392 – neon bright pink
- ✢ Metallic threads:
- • Mettler
  - #5833 – green

Prepping and Designing

1. Trace the patterns and prep the fabrics as described on page 21. Assemble the multiple parts of an element (examples: iris, lily, etc.) prior to final placement.

2. Remove any backing paper and lay out your design on the background fabric, using the pattern as a guide. Remember to allow for the ¼" (0.6cm) seam allowance on the sides of the background fabric. When happy with the placement and design, iron the appliqué pieces (with pressing cloth placed over the pieces) into position to adhere to the background fabric.

Joining the Blocks

1. Pin the sashing to the left side of the background fabric (with right sides together). Sew together with a ¼" (0.6cm) seam allowance.

2. Iron the seam allowance to sashing side.

3. Pin the sashing (and Block 2) to the right-side placement line of Block 1 (with right sides together). Remember to place the sashing ¼" (0.6cm) above and below the squared markings.

4. Sew the sashing to the batting and muslin with a ¼" (0.6cm) seam allowance.

Block 2 layout diagram.

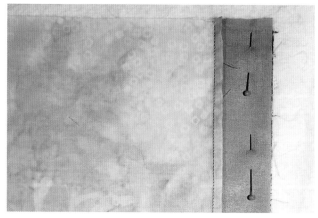

The sashing needs to be placed ¼" (0.6cm) above and below the squared markings to allow for a seam allowance.

Starting in the far-left center of Block 2, quilt up to the top and down to the bottom and make your way to the right edge. Don't forget those little background areas in between the elements of the design!

5. Flip the sashing and Block 2 over and iron flat. Check to make sure the batting and muslin remain bump-free. Pin in place, ensuring the sashing and blocks look straight.

6. With Poly Sheen thread (matching the color of the sashing), sew ⅛" (0.3cm) topstitch on both inside lines of the sashing. This will secure the pieces and help keep the sashing and blocks straight.

7. Free motion quilt the background, following the instructions on page 23. Start from the far-left side center of Block 2. Work your way to the top and bottom of the block and toward the right edge of the background fabric.

Thread Painting

Leaving your feed dogs down, and your free-motion foot on, switch the needle on your machine to a Topstitch 90/14 needle.

BASE STITCHING

Set your machine to a zigzag stitch with a width of 2.0 and length of 0.0 (if the pieces are small, decrease the width to 1.5). For more information, see page 26.

Completed base stitching for Block 2.

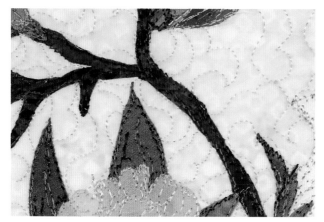

1. Branches. Using variegated dark brown thread, sew along the outer edges of the branches and add some detail stitching (such as wood grain) in the middle of the branches. Jump-stitch while sewing to get from one area of the branch to another section of the branch. Clip threads when finished.

3. Leaves. Use a variety of the variegated greens on the different leaves. Use one variegated green on one specific flower, such as variegated dark greens on all the leaves of the violets, variegated lime greens on all the lily leaves, etc. When you have multiple leaves within a block, using a single color for each type of leaf will keep your design uniform. Having several different variegated greens on the block will still create depth and separation of the different leaves. Follow the direction of the leaf patterns. For instance, the lily of the valley, lily, and iris leaves have long lined detailing but the violet and magnolia details come from the center vein with side branching.

2. Flowerpots. Use variegated medium brown thread. To create separation and difference in the two pots, sew one pot in one direction (horizontally) and the other pot in a different direction (vertically). Make sure you outline the edges, but also add some detail stitching in the middle of the pots. This helps to keep the area flat and free of bumps.

4. Dogwood flowers. Use variegated pinks. On each petal, sew along the edges and add additional stitching coming from the inner area on the petals (branching off from the center of each flower).

5. Lily, lily bud, and lily of the valley flowers. Use variegated pastels thread. For the lily and lily bud, sew along the outer edges and the edges of the center parts. (Samples might show yellow and pink fabrics used for center pieces—always use variegated pastels no matter what color fabric you use.) Also, add additional details in the direction and shape of the petals.

Before starting the lily-of-the-valley flowers, decrease the zigzag width to 1.5. Only outline and secure the edges. Since the pieces are so small, you need to be careful not to add too much threading during this step.

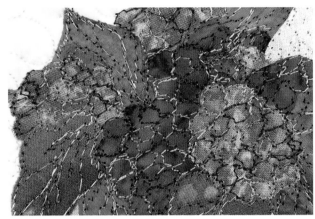

6. Violets. Use two different variegated purples. Only use one thread per floral piece. Sew in a circular motion to form individual clusters of five petals. Completely fill in each floral piece with the same colored thread.

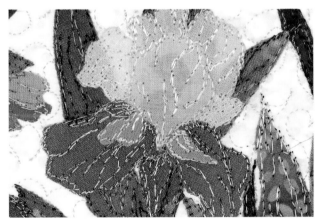

7. Iris. Use variegated purples and variegated yellows. On the purple petals, sew along the outer edges and add additional detail stitching to help form the shape and bend of the individual petals. On the yellow petals and mustard pieces, use variegated yellows. Sew the same stitching as on the purple petals.

8. Butterfly. Use variegated blue/black on the black fabrics and variegated blues on the blue fabrics. Decrease the zigzag stitch with to 1.5. Since all the parts are small, only outline and secure the outer edges.

ADDITIONAL STITCHING

Before you being adding more stitching, pause to iron your quilt. Treat Block 1, sashing, and Block 2 as a single unit and iron from the center, pressing up, down, and to both sides.

For the following steps, use a straight stitch and solid-colored threads. See page 27 for more details.

Completed thread painting on Block 2.

1. Branches. Use dark brown to add detail and shading onto the wood branches. Outline the edges and add additional stitches to create an impression of wood grain.

2. Flowerpots. Use four different brown thread colors (two medium and two dark) for the two pots. Use a different combination of two browns on each pot. Remember to add shading and highlighting in the same direction as the variegated stitching.

3. Leaves. Use multiple and different combinations of the numerous green threads, similar to what you did for the leaves in Block 1. Layer the threads for

I used a variety of green thread colors on the leaves.

additional shading and detail. It is important to follow the line patterns of detail for the different leaves. I used a total of seven threads.

For the lily-of-the-valley leaves, use #0092(medium green) for the shading and highlighting, followed by #0314 (dark green) for added detail, definition, and separation of the leaves.

For the magnolia leaves, use #1314 (medium green) for shading and highlighting, followed by #5833 (metallic green) for added sparkle. Finish with #0757 (dark green) for added detail, definition, and separation of the leaves.

For the lily and bud leaves, use #0224 (medium green) for shading and highlighting, followed by #0905 (dark green) for added detail, definition, and separation of the leaves.

For the spikes, use #0757 (dark green) to highlight and define the shape of each individual spike leaf.

For the violet leaves, use #0092 (medium green) for shading and highlighting, followed by #5833 (metallic green) for added sparkle, and finish with #0905 (dark green) for added detail, definition, and separation of the leaves.

The iris leaves use #0224 (medium green) for shading and highlighting, followed by #0314 (dark green) for added detail, definition, and separation of the leaves.

4. Iris and bud. Shade and blend with multiple colors to create a soft, natural appearance.

Use a medium purple to add shading to the tips of the purple petals, layering in two to three rows. The stitches should be irregular in length, with some being longer and some shorter. The next row should slightly overlap and mimic the same stitching.

Next, use a slightly lighter purple thread as a highlighting thread. Use this color to create the fall and bend of the petals.

Finally, use a dark purple thread to outline and define each petal. Also, use this thread color as a highlighting thread to make the lighter colors pop.

For the yellow petals, the stitching technique is done the same way as the purple petals, but with yellow threads instead of purple. Start with a medium yellow thread.

Next, use a light and bright yellow thread to highlight the petals. Apply as previously done with the slightly lighter purple thread.

Then add a mustard yellow thread on the tips and outline the yellow petals. Do the outlining with an irregular (almost shaky-looking) stitch to help create the ruffled appearance.

Lastly, use the same light purple thread (used on purple petals) to stitch the veining through the center yellow petal.

Tip

When you use the same light purple thread to create the veining on the yellow iris petals, you visually tie the two parts of the flower together and add interest.

5. Lily and bud. Use the white thread on all tips of the lily and bud. Layer the three shades of pink thread, from the lightest to the darkest (into the center). Remember to overlap the stitching, blending, and slightly overlap the prior threads. When finished, use the middle pink thread to outline and define each petal.

Add "dots" with dark brown thread. Change the machine setting to zigzag (1.5 width and 0.0 length) and stitch. Remain in place for numerous stitches, creating a buildup in the same area to form the appearance of small French knots.

Use a bright medium green to create the long, skinny parts of the stamens (filaments). Sew the lines multiple times, over and over, until achieving desired thickness. Use the yellow mustard thread to create the knobs at the end of the stamens (anthers). Change the machine setting to zigzag (2.0 width and 0.0 length) and stitch to form the appearance of a long French knot.

You can re-create the look of a French knot with a machine by using a zigzag stitch and keeping the needle in one spot for numerous stitches.

6. Magnolia. Use two threads, a medium pink and maroon. For the first step of shading on the flowers and buds, use a slightly darker pink thread than the actual fabric. Use this thread to highlight and add shape to the petals. I still like to see the fabric and variegated thread, as the additional colors help with the shading. Next, use a slightly dark pink or maroon to blend all the colors together. Also use maroon to outline and define the individual petals.

8. Lily of the valley. Use teal blue thread. Only stitch on the top area of the bell, leaving the bottom areas white. Start the shading from the top of the bell, finishing with outlining only on the top cap.

9. Butterfly. With black thread, clean up the stitching and outline the multiple pieces on the edges. Also add veining on the blue sections, and end with the antennas.

7. Violets. With the medium purple, outline the violet flower clusters. Follow this with the same stitching using the dark purple. Next, use the yellow thread for the flower centers. Change the machine setting to zigzag (1.5 width and 0.0 length) and stitch to form the appearance of a French knot.

Remember!

Iron the block and check for bumps and uneven quilting. If any issues appear, add some curlicues and grass spikes. Also, add some to balance the same whimsical and softness as in Block 1.

Blocking and Squaring

After completing all the quilting and thread painting, the block may look misshapen. Adding Block 3 and squaring up the unit will help correct this issue.

BLOCKING

Before beginning, make sure the entire area for ironing is flat and able to get wet from the steam of the iron.

Follow the same process outlined in Block 1 (page 41), paying special attention to the areas where Block 3 will be placed.

SQUARING

Once completely dry, square up the quilt and prepare to add the bottom sashing and Block 3.

1. Place the largest ruler or rulers on the combined Block 1/Block 2 unit. Work off as many horizontal and vertical lines on the blocks and sashing as possible (trellis lines, basket handle, sashing, and flowerpot lines). Use these reference lines to aide in squaring of the unit.

2. When everything looks as straight as possible, mark a straight placement line across the bottom of the Block 1/Block 2 unit. Make sure that all batting will be covered when adding the sashing. This new line is the placement line for adding the next sashing and Block 3.

3. The Block 1/Block 2 unit is squared and marked at the bottom. The line indicates where you'll add the next sashing and Block 3. From the marked lines, measure the width and length of the block in several places to check to make sure the measurements are all the same. These lines are the foundation for future blocks, so it's important to make sure they're straight.

4. Measure from the left vertical marking line of Block 1 to the outer edge of Block 2. Measurements should be approximately 31½" (80cm) in length. (If your measurements are slightly different, that is okay! You will adjust your future measures for your quilt.)

When adding the line at the bottom of the Block 1/Block 2 unit, be sure that all the batting will be covered when the sashing is added.

CHAPTER 6

Summer Visitors

Block 3

MATERIALS

- ✤ Pattern, page 110
- ✤ Background: light green batik, cut to 32" x 10" (81.3 x 25.4cm)
- ✤ Sashing: light blue batik, cut to 32" x 2" (81.3 x 5.1cm)
- ✤ Freezer paper
- ✤ Appliqué fabric suggestions: batiks and ombré cottons, in tan, medium blue, rust, yellow, light blue, medium blue, dark blue, black, light purple, medium purple, 3–4 mixed greens, light orange, medium orange, and 2–3 medium pinks
- • **Fence:** tan (#1); make 9

- • **Rail:** tan; cut 1½" x 26" (rough-cut edges to mimic a broken fence post)
- • **Bird:** medium blue (#2, #3, and #5) and rust (#4)
- • **Butterflies:** yellow (#6 and #7) (#11–14), blue (#8 and #9) (#15, #16–18), and black (#10 and #19)
- • **Coneflowers:** purple (#20 and #21), yellow (#22 and #23), and mixed greens (#24–26); make 5 flowers and 5–8 leaves
- • **Cornflower leaves:** mixed greens (#24, #25, and #26); make 5–8
- • **Ivy:** mixed greens (#27–30); make 20

- • **Delphiniums:** light blue (#31–36), medium blue (#37–42), dark blue (#43–48), and green (#49–51); make 5 of each petal shape and 12–14 leaves
- • Delphinium leaves: green (#49–51); make 12–14
- • **Zinnias**
  Flowers: Mixed pinks, oranges, purples and yellows for flower A (#52–56), flower B (#57 and #58), flower C (#59 and #60), and flower D (#61–63); make 7 flowers total and 1 bud
  Leaves: mixed greens (#64–66); make 15–17

THREADS

- ✤ Background: Mettler Poly Sheen (match the color of the fabric)
- ✤ Variegated threads:
- • Mettler Silk Finish Cotton 50 Multi
  - #9855 – mixed tans
  - #9818 – mixed dark greens
  - #9817 – mixed lime green
  - #9827 – mixed yellows
  - #9848 – mixed reds
  - #9838 – mixed purples
  - #9813 – mixed blues and black
- • Mettler Poly Sheen Multi
  - #9932 – mixed greens
  - #9930 – mixed blues
  - #9924 – mixed oranges
  - #9923 – mixed pinks

- ✤ Solid-colored threads:
- • Mettler Silk Finish Cotton 50
  - #0832 – medium brown
  - #0263 – dark brown
  - #0380 – tan
  - #0224 – medium green
  - #0314 – dark blue green
  - #0092 – medium green
  - #1314 – medium green
  - #0757 – dark green
  - #0905 – dark green
  - #0024 – dark teal blue
  - #1085 – medium lilac
  - #1062 – medium magenta
  - #0046 – dark purple
  - #2263 – yellow
  - #0608 – mustard yellow
  - #0163 – light rust

  - #4000 – black
  - #1334 – orange
  - #0122 – light orange
  - #1074 – rust
  - #3000 – white
  - #0339 – medium blue
  - #1394 – medium teal
  - #1423 – medium pink
  - #1392 – medium pink
  - #0067 – light pink
  - #0869 – maroon
  - #0029 – lilac
  - #1085 – medium lilac
  - #0790 – medium orange
- ✤ Metallic thread:
- • Mettler
  - #5833 – green

Prepping and Designing

1. With right sides together, sew the sashing and Block 3 background together; use a ¼" (0.6cm) seam allowance. Iron the sashing and background, pressing the seam toward the sashing.

2. Design Block 3 as suggested. When placing pieces along the bottom edge, take into consideration that you will be adding sashing onto the bottom and sides of the block at a later step.

   Remember to balance the design and have the same open spacing between the fence post and on the sides. When happy with the placement and design, iron the appliqué pieces (with a pressing cloth placed over the pieces) in place to adhere to the background fabric.

Joining Blocks

1. Pin sashing (and Block 3) with right sides together on the placement line of the Block 1/Block 2 unit. Remember to place the sashing ¼" (0.64cm) over on each side the squared markings.

2. Sew the sashing to the batting and muslin with a ¼" (0.6cm) seam allowance.

3. Flip the sashing and Block 3 over and iron flat. Check to make sure the batting and muslin remain free of bumps. Pin in place, ensuring the sashing and all three blocks look straight.

4. With Poly Sheen thread (matching the color of the sashing), topstitch ⅛" (0.3cm) along both inside lines of the sashing. This will secure and help keep the sashing and blocks straight.

5. Free motion quilt the background using the instructions on page 23. Start from the top center of Block 3. Work your way to each side of the block, while moving down to the bottom of the block.

Tip

It is very helpful to have extra leaves to tuck into empty spaces and soften the overall appearance. When laying out the designs, overlap the flowers petals and leaves, tucking behind and in front of the fence and other flowers to create a natural appearance.

Thread Painting

Leaving your feed dogs down, and your free-motion foot on, switch the needle on your machine to a Topstitch 90/14 needle.

BASE STITCHING

Set your machine to a zigzag stitch with a width of 2.0 and length of 0.0 (if the pieces are small, decrease the width to 1.5). For more information, see page 26.

1. Fence. Use variegated tan threads. Sew along the outer edges of the fence parts, adding detailed stitching in the middle to create wood grain. Remember to sew in the correct direction of the fence parts. For instance, sew the posts with lines going up and down.

2. Leaves. Although you will use a variety of the variegated green threads on the different leaves, only use one variegated green thread on one specific flower's leaf. For example, use the variegated dark greens on all the leaves of the zinnias, variegated lime greens on all the coneflower leaves, etc. With so many different leaves on one block, it helps to have a uniform look on each specific floral design. Having several different variegated greens on the block creates depth and separation of the different leaves.

Here is Block 3 with the base stitching completed.

3. Delphiniums. Decrease the zigzag width to 1.5. Only outline and secure the edges on each petal with variegated blue thread. Since the pieces are so small, you need to be careful not to add too much threading on this step.

4. Zinnias. Use an assortment of variegated threads on the petals and centers. Match the pink, red, and orange petals and yellow and purple centers with the appropriate thread colors. On the petals, stitch along the edges and inside the petal to add color. In the center, with circular stitching, sew along the edges and inside the middle.

5. Purple coneflowers. Use a variegated purple thread for the petals and variegated yellow thread for the centers. Follow the same stitching as the zinnias.

6. Bird. Decrease the zigzag width to 1.5. Use variegated blue thread on the blue areas and variegated orange thread on belly area. Stitching in the direction of the feathers and sewing on all the outer edges of all the pieces.

7. Butterflies. Decrease the zigzag stitch width to 1.5. Use variegated blue/black thread on the black fabrics and variegated yellow thread on the yellow fabrics. Since all the parts are small, only outline and secure the outer edges.

ADDITIONAL STITCHING

Iron the quilt from the middle of the new unit (Block 1/Block 2/Block 3) pressing up, down, and to both sides. Approach the Block 1/Block 2/Block 3 unit as one whole unit.

For this section, use a straight stitch and solid-color threads. For more information, see page 27.

1. Fence. Use three brown threads. First, use a medium and dark brown thread, finishing with a light tan to highlight and create a "worn" fence appearance. Use medium-brown thread to add detail and shading on the wood. Create the wood grain in the correct direction. Next, use the dark brown thread to shade and outline all the posts to define the edges. Lastly, use the tan thread to add more detail and highlighting. Do not forget all the little pieces of fencing behind the flowers!

2. Leaves. Use multiple and different combinations of the numerous green. Layer the threads for additional shading and detail. It is important to follow the line patterns of detail for the different leaves. Suggestions for threading combinations on leaves are as follow (using a total of seven threads).

For the delphiniums, use #0224 (medium green) for shading and highlighting, followed by #0314 (dark blue green) for added detail and definition of the leaves.

Remember!

I do not try to avoid or purposely sew on the variegated threads. I add these additional solid-colored threads to blend and add to the thread work.

This is what Block 4 looks like with all of the thread painting finished.

When thread painting the coneflowers, use #0092 for shading and highlighting, followed by #5833 (metallic green) for some sparkle. Finish with #0757 (dark green) for added detail, definition, and separation of the leaves.

To complete the zinnias, use #1314 (medium green) for shading and highlighting, followed by #0757 (dark green) for added detail and definition of the leaves.

For the ivy, use #0092 (medium green) for shading and highlighting, followed by #5833 (metallic green) for some sparkle. Finish with #0757 (dark green) for added detail, definition, and separation of the leaves.

a slightly darker purple thread than the actual fabric. Use this thread to highlight and add shape to the petals. Next, use a medium magenta to highlight and blend all the colors together. Finally, use dark purple to outline and define the individual petals.

Create the flower centers' spiky and ombré appearance by layering the threads from the top with the lightest yellow thread and overlapping in the middle with a slightly darker yellow thread. Finish at the bottom with light rust spikes.

5. Zinnias. Work the petals the same way as done with the variegated threads during the base stitching. (This technique is also similar to the stitching done on the purple coneflowers.) Match the pink, red, and orange petals and yellow and purple centers with the appropriate solid-colored thread combinations. On each petal, sew along the edges and add stitching from the inner area on the petals (branching off from the center of each flower).

For the pink zinnias, use #1423 (medium pink) for shading along the edges and tips of the petals. This will be followed by #1392 (medium pink) to add more shading. Next, use #0067 (light pink) to add highlighting onto the tips and edges of the petals. Finish with #0869 (maroon) to outline and define each petal.

3. Delphiniums. Use dark teal-blue thread. Stitch the outer edges of each bell, then form an inner line to create the appearance of the tube shape of each petal. Add additional shading from the center of the bell where it is attached to the stem.

4. Purple coneflowers. Use three thread colors for the petals: medium lilac, medium magenta, and dark purple. For the first step of shading on the petals, use

For the pink/orange combination zinnias, use the same stitching technique as done on the pink zinnias. Use #1392 (medium pink) on the pink areas, followed by #0790 (medium orange) on the orange areas. Finish with #0869 (maroon).

To stitch the zinnia centers, repeat the same stitching technique as done on the coneflower centers.

For the purple centers, use #0029 (lilac) on the top, then finish with #1085 (medium lilac) on the bottom. The yellow centers will need #2263 (yellow) on the top before being finished with #0608 (dark yellow) on the bottom.

6. Butterflies. Use three threads to complete the butterflies. First, use #0608 (mustard gold) on the yellow areas to add shading and separation of the wings. Next, outline the blue sections with #0024 (dark teal blue) threads. Finally, use #4000 (black) thread on the edges to clean up the stitching and outline the multiple pieces, finishing with the antennas.

7. Bird. Many layers of small stitches, sewn in rows, create a soft blending and shading for the appearance of feathers on the bird. Start on the belly and work up the body and wings to the head. You'll want to overlap the stitching but also be mindful of the direction of the different body parts.

On the orange/rust area, use #0790 (medium orange) thread. Start from the bottom of the belly to the neck. Sew small stitches to imitate the layering of feathers. Use #0122 (light orange) to highlight the chest and belly areas close to the tail. Add #1074 (rust) along the edge of the chest, blending into the orange threads.

On the blue areas and completing details, add #3000 (white) on the tips of the wing and tail. Use #0339 (medium blue) along the tail, wing, and head areas. Overlap the stitches to blend the feathers together. Add #1394 (medium teal) to highlight the areas that need separation and a pop of color. Use #0024 (dark teal blue) to define and separate the different body parts. Also, add some more stitching in #0024 (dark teal blue) to blend and create feathers. Use #4000 (black) to add the eye with a small zigzag stitch sewn in place. With #0263 (dark brown) stitch the feet, making the bird look as if he is standing on the fence.

8. Press the block. Even if you have been using your iron on the block throughout the previous steps, press the block again!

9. Add grass spikes or curlicues. After completing all the thread painting on Block 3 (and ironing it flat), look for any raised bumps or areas of uneven treading or quilting. If there are any areas of concern, see step 11 on page 40.

Blocking and Squaring

BLOCKING

Press the entire unit flat, and make sure it will all get wet from the steam of the iron.

Follow the same process outlined in Block 1 (page 41), paying special attention to the areas where Block 4 will be placed.

SQUARING

Once completely dry, square up the quilt and prepare to add side sashing and Block 4.

1. Place the largest ruler on the Block 1/Block 2/ Block 3 unit. Work off as many horizontal and vertical lines on the blocks and sashing as possible (trellis lines, basket handle, fence post, and sashing). Use these reference lines to aide in squaring of the unit.

2. When everything looks as straight as possible, mark a straight placement line across the left side of the Block 1/Block 2/Block 3 unit. Make sure that all batting will be covered when adding the sashing. Remember, this new line is the placement line for adding the next sashing and Block 4. It's very important that these lines are straight since you'll be continue to expand the quilt one block at a time.

3. Measure from the top to the bottom left vertical marked line on Block 1 and Block 3. Measurements should be approximately 26½" (67.3cm) in length. (If your measurements are slightly different, that is okay. You will adjust your future measures for your quilt.)

This is what your quilt will look like when you've finished squaring it.

CHAPTER 7

Fall Delights

Block 4

MATERIALS

- ✛ Pattern, page 113
- ✛ Background: light green batik, cut to 27" x 11½" (68.6 x 29.2cm)
- ✛ Sashing: light blue batik, cut to 27" x 2" (68.6 x 5.1cm)
- ✛ Freezer paper
- ✛ Appliqué fabric suggestions: batiks and ombré cottons, in tan, medium brown, dark brown, medium blue, dark blue, 4–5 yellows, 4–5 greens, 3–5 pinks, 3–4 purples, rust, maroon, orange, red, gray, pale yellow, white, and black
- **Post:** tan (#1) cut to 14¾" x 2" (37.47 x 5.1cm)
- **House:** tan (#2 and #3), dark blue (#4), medium blue (#5), medium brown (#6 and #8), and dark brown (#7)
- **Sunflowers**
  Flowers: mixed yellows (#9–21) and brown (#22); make 2

- Bud: mixed yellows (#23–32) and medium green (#33–37)
  Leaves: 2–3 greens (#38–41); make 2 of each (total of 8)
- **Cosmos**
  Petals: mixed pinks for flower A (#42–49) and mixed pinks for flower B (#50–56); make 2 of each
  Centers: yellow (#57 and #58)
  Leaves: 2–3 greens (#59–61); make 4 of each
- **Buddleia**
  Flowers: mixed purples (#62–66); make 2–3 of each
  Leaves: dark green (#67–69); make 5 of each
- **Gaillardia**
  Flowers: yellow (#70–75), rust (#70a–75a), and maroon (#76); make 3 of each
  Bud: yellow (#77–80), rust (#77a–80a), and green (#81–84)

- **Asters**
  Petals: mixed purples (#85–87); make 3 large, 6 medium, and 1 small
  Centers: yellow (#88); make 9
  Leaves: green (#89–90); make 8
- **Small daisies:** yellow (#91), orange (#92), and green (#93); make 8 each of yellow and orange and make 12 of green
- **Branches and berries:** brown (#94 and #95) and red (#96); make as many as desired to fill the area
- **Bird:** gray (#98, #100, and #101), pale yellow (#99), white (#102), and brown (#103)
- **Butterfly:** black (#104–108) and blue (#104a–108a)

THREADS

✜ Background: Mettler Poly Sheen
(match the color of the fabric)
✜ Variegated threads:
● Mettler Silk Finished Cotton 50 Multi
  - #9818 – mixed dark green
  - #9817 – mixed lime greens
  - #9855 – mixed tans
  - #9852 – mixed dark blues
  - #9827 – mixed dark yellows
  - #9859 – mixed pale yellows
  - #9848 – mixed reds
  - #9838 – mixed purples
  - #9813 – mixed blues and black
  - #9812 – mixed medium blues
● Mettler Poly Sheen Multi
  - #9932 – mixed greens
  - #9924 – mixed oranges
  - #9923 – mixed pinks
  - #9912 – mixed light purples
  - #9930 – mixed light blues
✜ Solid-colored threads:
● Mettler Silk Finished Cottons 50
  - #1425 – medium brown
  - #0263 – dark brown
  - #1002 – dark brown
  - #0092 – medium green
  - #1314 – medium green
  - #0224 – medium green
  - #0757 – dark green
  - #0314 – dark green
  - #0608 – mustard yellow
  - #0163 – dark orange
  - #1074 – dark orange
  - #0264 – dark brown
  - #0899 – gold
  - #0263 – dark brown
  - #0869 – maroon
  - #0111 – dark maroon
  - #0076 – light pink
  - #1423 – medium pink
  - #1392 – medium pink
  - #2263 – yellow
  - #1394 – medium blue
  - #4000 – black
  - #1085 – medium purple
  - #1062 – medium magenta
  - #0046 – dark purple
  - #0029 – lilac
  - #1134 – orange
  - #3000 – white
  - #0415 – gray
  - #0348 – dark gray
✜ Metallic
● Mettler
  - #5833 – green
  - #2108 – gold

Here is the design layout for Block 4.

Prepping and Designing

1. With right sides together, sew the sashing and Block 4 background together; use a ¼" (0.6cm) seam allowance. Iron the sashing and background, pressing the seam toward the sashing.

2. Lay out Block 4 as suggested. When placing pieces along the left, top, and bottom, take into consideration you will be adding additional sashing around the block at a later step.

Remember to balance the design and leave the same spacing on each side. When happy with the placement and design, iron the appliqué pieces (with pressing cloth placed over the pieces) in place to adhere to the background fabric.

Tip

It is very helpful to have extra leaves to tuck into empty spaces and soften the overall appearance. When laying out the designs, overlap the flower petals and leaves. Tuck the extra leaves behind and in front of the post and other flowers to create a natural appearance.

Joining Blocks

1. Pin the sashing and Block 4 with right sides together on the placement line of Block 1 and Block 3. Remember to place the sashing ¼" (0.6cm) over on each side the squared markings.

2. Sew the sashing to the batting and muslin with a ¼" (0.6cm) seam allowance. Flip the sashing and Block 4 over and iron flat. Check to make sure the batting and muslin are free of bumps. Pin in place, ensuring the sashing and all four blocks look straight.

3. With Poly Sheen thread (matching the color of the sashing), sew ⅛" (0.3cm) topstitch line on both inside lines of the sashing. This will secure and help keep the sashing and blocks straight.

4. Free motion quilt the background , following the insructions on page 23. Start from the right center of Block 4 and work your way to the left side of the block, while moving up and down to the outer left edge of the block.

Follow the arrows in this image for the correct quilting direction.

Thread Painting

Leaving your feed dogs down, and your free-motion foot on, switch the needle on your machine to a Topstitch 90/14 needle.

BASE STITCHING

Set your machine to a zigzag stitch with a width of 2.0 and length of 0.0 (if the pieces are small, decrease the width to 1.5). For more information, see page 26.

1. **Birdhouse.** Use variegated tan threads on the wood post and main house parts. Sew along the outer edges of the post and brown house parts. Add detailed stitching in the middle to create wood grain (similar to fence on Block 3; see page 56).

    For the hole and perch parts, use variegated dark brown threads.

    For the roof parts, use variegated dark blue threads. Create stitches very similar to the type made in the brown areas, following the roofline.

Remember!

Change the bobbin thread to match the color family of the thread on top.

2. Leaves. Be sure to use a variety of the variegated green thread on the different leaves. As in prior blocks, maintain uniformity on each specific floral design by using one variegated green thread on one specific flower (see page 56).

3. Branches. With a variegated dark brown thread, sew along the outer edges and add some detail stitching (such as wood grain) in the middle of the branches. Jump-stitch while sewing to get from one area of the branch to another section of the branch. Clip threads when finished.

4. Sunflowers. This uses similar stitching as used for the purple coneflowers in Block 3 (see page 57). Use a variegated yellow thread on the petals. Stitch along the edges and inside the petals to add color. For the flower centers, use variegated brown thread, sewn in a circular motion, along the edges and filling in the inside.

5. Cosmos. This uses similar stitching as done in the sunflowers in the previous step. Use a variegated pink thread for the petals. Stitch along the edges and inside the petals to add color. For the flower centers, use variegated yellow thread, sewn in a circular motion, along the edges and filling in the inside.

Remember!

Sew in the correct direction of the different parts. For example, sew the post with vertical lines.

6. Buddleia. Use two variegated purple-colored threads on the flowers. Sew each flower with longer, more elongated ovals that fill in the area and cover the outer edges. Only use one variegated purple thread per flower.

8. Small daisies. Decrease the zigzag stitch width to 1.5. For the petals, use a variegated pale yellow thread. Sew each flower along the edges and inside the petals to add color.

For the flower centers, use variegated yellow thread, sewn in circular motion, only along the edges.

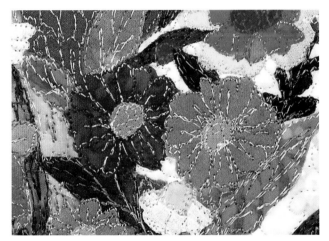

7. Asters. Use two variegated purples on the flower petals. Each flower is sewn along the edges and inside the petals to add color. Only use one variegated purple thread per flower.

For the flower centers, use a variegated yellow thread, sewn in a circular motion, along the edges and filling in the inside.

9. Gaillardia and buds. Decrease the zigzag stitch width to 1.5. Use a pale yellow variegated thread only on the outer edges of the outer petals.

Use a variegated orange thread for the inner petals, sewing very similar to the stitching of the aster petals in step 7.

For the flower centers, use a variegated red thread, sewn in a circular motion, along the edges and filling in the insides.

10. Berries. Decrease the zigzag stitch width to 1.5. Use a variegated red thread, sewn in a circular motion along the edges and fill inside the middle.

11. Butterfly. Decrease the zigzag stitch width to 1.5. Use a variegated blue/black thread on the black fabrics and variegated blue thread on the blue fabrics. Since all the parts are small, only outline and secure the outer edges.

12. Bird. Decrease the zigzag width to 1.5. Use a variegated blue/black thread on the black areas and variegated pale yellow thread on the belly area. Stitch in the direction of the feathers and sew on all the outer edges of all the pieces.

ADDITIONAL STITCHING

Press the quilt, ironing from the middle of the new unit, moving from the center, pressing up, down, and to both sides.

For this section, use a straight stitch and solid-color threads. For more information, see page 27.

1. Birdhouse. For the tan/brown parts, use three brown threads. First, use two medium and dark brown threads to create a wood-grain appearance. Use medium brown thread to add detail and shading on the wood. Create the wood grain in the correct direction.

Next, use another medium (slightly darker) brown thread to shade, outline, and define the post and house.

Lastly, use the very dark thread to add more detail and define the shape of the house. Also, outline the "hole" and "perch." Do not forget all the little pieces of the post behind the leaves and flowers.

Use medium and dark blue threads for shading and defining the different parts of the blue roof. Make sure the stitching follows the correct direction and pitch of the roof. Add medium blue thread to create a highlight and to brighten the roof's appearance. Next, add the dark blue to separate the underlining roof pieces.

2. **Leaves.** Use multiple and different combinations of the numerous green threads. This will be similar to the same combinations of green threads used on Block 2 (page 48) and Block 3 (page 58). Layer the threads for additional shading and detail. It is important to follow the line patterns of detail for the different leaves. See Block 2 and Block 3 for possible thread combinations or create new ones!

3. **Tree branches and berries.** First, use a dark brown thread to add detail and shading on the wood

Block 4 with completed thread painting.

branches. Outline the edges and add stitches to create the impression of wood grain. Next, use two shades of maroon for the berries. Add the medium maroon to shade, highlight, and shape the berries. Then add the dark maroon to outline and separate the berries where they touch each other or the wood branches.

4. Sunflowers. Layer the four shades of yellow to orange, from the lightest to the darkest (in the center). Remember to connect the stitching, blending and slightly overlapping the previous threads.

The threads in my piece were layered using #0608 (mustard gold) first, adding #2108 (metallic gold) for some sparkle and highlighting, then building the colors and shading with #0163 (medium orange). Finish with #1074 (dark orange) for the center shading. Use the dark brown thread to outline, define, and separate each petal.

For the sunflower centers, multiple layers and three colors are used for the shading and blending of the threads to create a textured and natural appearance on the sunflower centers. Sew the layers in long- and irregular-length stitches, overlapping in different directions with the three different threads and blending them together. Start the shading in the center, stitching out to the edges. Begin with the lightest brown thread, layering with the medium brown, before finishing with the darkest brown.

5. Buddleias. Sew the layers in small and irregular length stitches, overlapping the different threads and blending them together. The majority of the shading comes from the center of the petals. Start with the lighter lilac thread layering before finishing with the darker purple in the innermost center of each petal.

First, use the lilac thread on the tips of each oval within the flower cluster. Then layer the two other shades of purple threads from the lightest to the darkest (into the center of each petal). Remember to connect the stitching, blending and slightly overlapping the prior threads. Use the darkest purple thread to outline and define each petal within the clusters.

Tip

Sew in multiple layers with three different purple threads to shade and blend the colors. This creates a soft and natural appearance in each cluster of petals.

6. Gaillardias and bud. Sew the individual pieces separately. The majority of the shading comes from the inner area of the petals.

Use the mustard yellow thread on the tips of the yellow area. Sew with irregular and short stitches. With an "irregular-length zigzag" stitch, create a jagged edge. Use a dark orange thread to outline the tips and separate each petal.

For the red areas, use a slightly darker orange than used in the yellow areas, but repeat the same stitching technique. Use a medium to dark maroon to outline the tips and separate each petal.

Use the dark maroon thread to outline and define the flower center, and blend into the red fabric areas.

7. Cosmos. The stitch technique for the cosmos is similar to the stitching done on the purple coneflowers and zinnias on Block 3 (see page 59). Here are my thread color suggestions: #1423 (medium pink) for shading along edges and tip of petals, followed by ##1392 (medium/dark pink) to add shading. Next, use #0067 (light pink) to add

highlights on the tips and edges. Finish with #0869 (maroon) to outline and define each petal.

Create the spiky and ombré appearance of the flower centers by layering and creating a spiky appearance with the threads all along the center's outer edge. Start with yellow thread, then overlap it in the middle with a slightly darker shade of yellow.

8. Asters. These flowers are completed with the same stitching technique as used for step 7 above. The only difference is that you use two threads and different color combinations. For the petals, use lilac and dark purple thread. For the centers, use the same color combination and layering as with the cosmos.

9. Small daisies. Use a similar method as the asters and cosmos in this block. Like the asters, use two threads and different color combinations. For the petals use dark yellow and orange thread. Since the pieces are smaller, be mindful not to add too many threads. The centers are created with orange and dark orange threads. Layer the stitching in a similar manner as with the purple coneflowers in Block 3 (see page 59).

10. Butterfly. Use black thread on the edges to clean up the stitching and outline the multiple pieces. Also, add veining on the blue sections, finishing with the antennas.

11. Bird. Many layers of small stitches, sewn in rows, create a soft blending and shading for the appearance of feathers on the bird. It is best to start from the belly, working up the body and wings to the head. Overlap the stitching but also be mindful of the direction of the different body parts.

For the yellow area, use white thread, starting from the bottom of the belly and moving along the neck areas. Sew small stitches to imitate the layering of feathers. Add light yellow thread to highlight the chest and belly area.

On the gray/black areas and completing details, add medium gray along the tail and wing areas. Overlap the stitches to blend the feathers together. Add dark gray thread to highlight areas that need separation and a pop of color. Add white thread along the edges of the wings and tail, blending with other threads to create feathers. Use black thread to define and shade the wings, head, beak, and arch of the neck and back. Lastly, add the eye with a small zigzag stitch, sewn in place.

12. Press. Even if you have been ironing the block throughout the above steps, press the block again!

13. Add twigs, grass spikes, or curlicues. Look for any raised bumps or uneven treading or quilting. If there are any areas of concern, add quilting or the twigs from the branches, grass spikes, or curlicues. See step 11 on page 40 for more instruction.

Blocking and Squaring

BLOCKING
Before beginning, make sure the entire area for ironing is flat and will get wet from the steam of the iron.

Follow the same process outlined in Block 1 (page 41), paying special attention to the areas where Blocks 5 and 6 will be placed.

SQUARING
Once completely dry, square the quilt and prepare to add side sashing and Blocks 5 and 6.

1. Place the largest ruler on Block 1, Block 2, Block 4, and sashing units. Work off as many horizontal and vertical lines on the blocks and sashing as possible (trellis lines, basket handle, birdhouse, and sashing pieces). Use these reference lines to aide in squaring of the unit.

2. When everything looks as straight as possible, mark an even placement line across the top line of Block 1, Block 2, and Block 4. Make sure that all the batting will be covered when adding the sashing. This new line is the placement line for adding the next sashing and Blocks 5 and 6.

3. Measure the squaring line from the top outer left edge of Block 4 to outer right edge of Block 2. Measurements should be approximately 41" (104.1cm) in length. (If your measurements are slightly different, that is okay. Cut to your measurements.)

The quilt now contains Blocks 1–4 and their sashing pieces.

CHAPTER 8

Garden's Harvest and Blooming Winter

Blocks 5 and 6

MATERIALS (BLOCK 5)

+ Pattern, page 117
+ Background: light green batik, cut to 23" x 10" (58.4 x 25.4cm)
+ Sashing: light blue batik, cut to 41" x 2" (104.1 x 5.1cm)
+ Appliqué fabric suggestions: batiks and ombré cottons, in light brown, medium brown, dark brown, 4–6 greens, medium blue, 4–5 yellows, ivory, 3–4 purples, 2–3 oranges, dark orange, red, and black
  • **Board:** light brown, cut 1 piece to 1¾" x 18½" (4.5 x 47cm)
  • **Rope:** light brown, cut 2 pieces to ¾" x 6¾" (2 x 17.2cm)
  • **Pegs:** medium brown (#1), make 6
  • **Mini black-eyed Susans**
    Leaves and stems: 2–3 greens (#2–6); make approx. 12–14 leaves and 5–6 stems
    Ribbon: medium blue (#7–9)
    Petals: medium yellow (#10); make 14–15

Centers: medium brown (#11); make 14–15
Tag: ivory (#12)
  • **Lilac**
    Leaves and stems: (#13–15) 2–3 greens (#13–15); make approx. 10 leaves and 4–5 stems
    Petal clusters: 3–4 purples (#16–18); make 5 of each color
    Tag: ivory (#19)
    Ribbon: medium blue (#20–22)
  • **Sunflowers**
    Leaves and stems: green (#23–24); make 3 large and 2 small for a total of 5 (use extra stem pieces from lilac)
    Tag: ivory (#25)
    Ribbon: medium blue (#26–28)
    Petals: 3–4 yellows (#29–41); make 2 of each piece to create 2 flowers
    Center: medium brown (#42); make 2

  • **Gomphrena globe flower**
    Leaves and stems: 2 medium greens (#43–45); make 12 leaves
    Flower: 2–3 oranges (#46); make 14–15
    Tag: ivory (#47)
    Ribbon: medium blue (#48–50)
  • **Aster**
    Stems: 2 greens (#51–53)
    Leaves: 2 greens (#54–55); make approx. 10–12 leaves
    Tag: ivory (#56)
    Ribbon: medium blue (#57–59)
    Flowers: purple (#60) and yellow (#61); make 14
    Buds: green (#62) and purple (#63); make 3
  • **Holly:** green (#64); make 3
  • **Cardinal:** red (#65–66), black (#67), and dark orange (#68)

MATERIALS (BLOCK 6)

+ Patterns, page 120
+ Background: light green batik, cut to 17" x 10" (43.2 x 25.4cm)
+ Sashing: light blue batik, cut to 10" x 2" (25.4 x 5.1cm)
+ Freezer paper
+ Appliqué fabric suggestions: batiks and ombré cottons, in light and medium orange, 2 medium greens, dark green, white, 2 yellows, dark purple, medium purple, dark gray, and light blue
  • **Fall leaves:** orange /browns (#1–3); make 2 of each

  • **Holly:** medium green (#4)
  • **Snow mound:** white (#5 and #6); make 2 of each
  • **Primroses**
    Flowers and buds: yellow (#7 and #8) and brown (#9); make 4 flowers and 2 buds
    Leaves: green (#10); make 5
  • **Crocus:** purple (#11), yellow (#12), and medium purple (#13); make 4 flowers; green (#14–16); make 2 each
  • **Bird:** dark gray (#17–18), white (#19), and yellow (#20)

  • **Daffodils**
    Leaves and stems: medium green (#21–26)
    Bud: yellow (#27); make 2
    Flower A: yellow (#28), light orange (#29), and orange (#30); make 2
    Flower B: yellow (#31), light orange (#32), and orange (#33); make 1
  • **Snow drops**
    Leaves and spikes: green (#34–41); make 2–3 to fill spaces
    Flower: light blue (#42 and #43) and white (#44 and #45); make total of 7

*Add, design, and sew Block 5 (top) and Block 6 (bottom)
together at the same time. This helps to maintain the
straight lines and prevent distortion in the upper areas of
the quilt.*

Tip

When creating the
different stems, make
enough pieces to
form a solid
bunch.

THREADS FOR BLOCK 5 AND BLOCK 6

✛ Background: Mettler Poly Sheen
(match the color of the fabric)

✛ Variegated threads:

• Mettler Silk Finished Cotton
50 Multi
- #9855 – mixed tans
- #9852 – mixed browns
- #9818 – mixed dark greens
- #9817 – mixed lime greens
- #9827 – mixed yellows
- #9838 – mixed purples
- #9848 – mixed reds
- #9813 – mixed blue/blacks
- #9859 – mixed pale yellows
- #9858 – mixed oranges

• Mettler Poly Sheen Multi
- #9932 – mixed greens
- #9924 – mixed oranges
- #9935 – mixed pastels
- #9930 – mixed blues

✛ Solid-colored threads:

• Silk Finished Solid 50 Cotton
- #3000 – white
- #1425 – tan
- #0263 – medium dark brown
- #0264 – dark brown
- #1002 – dark Brown
- #0092 – medium green
- #1314 – medium green
- #0224 – medium green
- #0314 – dark green
- #0757 – dark green
- #0905 – dark green
- #0608 – mustard
- #0163 – dark orange
- #1074 – rust
- #1334 – orange
- #0790 – bright orange
- #0105 – red
- #0029 – medium purple
- #1085 – medium purple
- #1062 – medium magenta
- #0046 – dark purple
- #0120 – yellow

- #1394 – medium blue
- #0024 – dark blue
- #0415 – medium gray
- #0869 – medium magenta
- #0111 – maroon
- #4000 – black
- #1440 – pale blue
- #0339 – medium blue
- #2522 – yellow
- #0046 – dark purple
- #0120 – yellow
- #2263 – yellow
- #1533 – dark yellow
- #0122 – peach
- #0415 – light gray
- #0416 – medium gray
- #0348 – dark gray
- #3507 – yellow

✛ Metallic:

• Mettler
- #5833 – green
- #2108 – gold

• Superior Threads Razzle Dazzle
- #251 – Icicles

Joining the Blocks

1. With right sides together, place the sashing piece for Block 5 to the right edge of Block 5. Sew together using a ¼" (0.6cm) seam allowance.

2. With right sides together, sew the sashing (and Block 5) to the left side of the Block 6 background. Use a ¼" (0.6cm) seam allowance.

3. Iron the sashing and backgrounds, pressing the seams inward toward the sashing.

4. With right sides together; place the long sashing piece evenly on the bottom of Block 5 and Block 6. Sew the long sashing piece to the bottom edge of the Block 5/Block 6 unit. Sew together using a ¼" (0.6cm) seam allowance. Press the seams inward toward the sashing.

5. Approach sewing and designing Block 5 and Block 6 (with both sashing pieces attached) as one unit. On both sides of this new unit, even up and trim the sashing or background fabric if needed.

6. With right sides together, evenly place the long sashing edge on the placement line of Blocks 1, 2, and 4. Center the Block 5/Block 6 unit with the Block 1/Block 2/Block 3/Block 4 unit. It is okay if these two units are slightly different in size! Pin in place.

7. Sew along the long sashing line, using a ¼" (0.6cm) seam allowance. Press seams toward the sashing.

8. Flip Block 5/Block 6 up. Press the blocks and sashing flat. Check that the layering of the muslin, batting, and top fabrics are flat and have no bumps or pleats. Make sure the vertical (between Blocks 5 and 6) and horizontal sashing pieces are straight. Pinning in place is very helpful.

9. With Poly Sheen thread (matching the color of the sashing), sew a ⅛" (0.3cm) topstitch line on both the inside lines of the two new sashing pieces. This secures and keeps the sashing and blocks straight. First sew the horizontal sashing, then the vertical sashing between Block 5 and Block 6.

Designing the Blocks

1. Layout Block 5 and Block 6 as suggested. When placing pieces along the sides, top, and bottom, remember that you will be adding sashing onto the sides and top of the blocks at a later step.

Balance the design and have the same spacing on each side. When happy with the placement and design, iron the appliqué pieces (with pressing cloth placed over the pieces) in place to adhere to the background fabric.

2. Free motion quilt the background fabrics on Blocks 5 and 6, following the instructions on page 23.

On Block 5, start from the bottom right corner and push your way up and over to the left side and top of the block.

On Block 6, start from the bottom left corner and push your way up and out to the right side and top of the block.

This is the design layout for Block 5.

Tip

The steps for prepping and designing and adding the sashing are a little different for Blocks 5 and 6. Unlike with previous blocks, we will be adding the sashing and sewing all units together before we design Blocks 5 and 6.

This is the design layout for Block 6 (also including the background quilting; see step 2).

Thread Painting

Leaving your feed dogs down, and your free-motion foot on, switch the needle on your machine to a Topstitch 90/14 needle.

BASE STITCHING
Set your machine for a zigzag stitch width of 2.0 and length of 0.0, and (if the pieces are small, decrease the width to 1.5). For more information, see page 26.

Block 5

Here is the base stitching for the black-eyed Susans, lilacs, sunflowers, and cardinal in Block 5.

1. **Board, pegs, and rope.** Use variegated tan threads. Sew along the outer edges of the fence parts. Add detailed stitching in the middle to create wood grain. Remember to sew in the correct direction of the fence parts. For example, sew the shelf with horizontal lines.

2. **Leaves.** Use a variety of the variegated green thread on the different leaves. As in prior blocks, use one variegated green thread on one specific flower for a more uniform design. For instance, use variegated dark greens on all the leaves of the sunflowers, use variegated lime greens on all the lilac leaves, etc. Having several different variegated greens on the block will still create depth and separation of the different leaves.

3. **Sunflowers.** First, use a variegated yellow thread on the petals. Stitch along the edges and inside the petal to add color. Next, use variegated brown thread on the center, sewn in a circular motion, along the edges and filling in the inside.

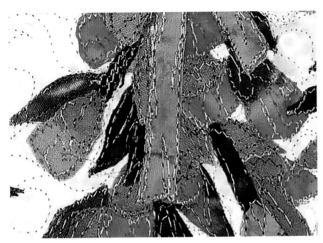

4. Gomphrena globe flower. Use variegated oranges, sewn in a circular motion, along the edges and filling in the inside.

5. Lilac. Use two variegated purples on the flowers and variegated greens on the leaves and stems. The flowers are sewn with small circles, filling in the area. Only use one purple thread per flower.

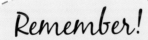

Remember!

Change the bobbin threads to match the color family used on top.

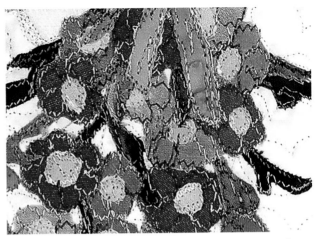

6. Asters. On the flower petals, use two variegated purples. First, each flower is sewn along the edges and inside the petals to add color. Only use one variegated purple thread per flower. Next, the flower centers are sewn in a circular motion with variegated yellow thread along the edges and filling in the inside.

7. Black-eyed Susans. Decrease the zigzag stitch with to 1.5. Use variegated yellows on the petals. Each flower is sewn along the edges and inside the petals to add color. Then use variegated brown thread for the flower centers, sewn in a circular motion, only along the edges.

8. Tags. Decrease the zigzag stitch with to 1.5. Use variegated pastels and sew along the outer edges only.

9. Ribbons. Decrease the zigzag stitch width to 1.5. Use variegated blues and sew along the outer edges of the branches. Add some detail stitching in the middle of the ribbon pieces.

10. Bird. Decrease the zigzag width to 1.5. Use variegated blues and black thread on the black areas and variegated red thread on red areas. Use variegated orange on the beak. Stitch in the direction of the feathers and sew on all the outer edges of all the pieces.

Block 6

Here is the completed base stitching for Block 6.

1. Flower leaves and holly. As with previous blocks, you will use a variety of the variegated green thread on the different leaves, sticking to one color for each flower type. Use variegated oranges on the fall leaves.

2. Snow. Use #3000 (white) thread. Sew along the outer edges and add some stitching in the middle for added texture.

3. Snowdrops. Decrease the zigzag width to 1.5. Use variegated blues. Only outline and secure the edges. Since the pieces are so small, be careful not to add too much threading on this step.

4. Crocuses. Use variegated purple on the petals and variegated yellows on the flower centers. On the petals, stitch along the edges and insides to add color. In the center, sew along the edges and inside the middle.

5. Daffodils. Use variegated dark yellows and variegated oranges. On the yellow petals, stitch along the edges and inside the petal to add color. On the orange petals, sew along the edges and inside the middle cup area.

6. **Primroses.** Use variegated pale yellows. Stitch along the edges and inside the center to add color.

7. **Bird.** Decrease the zigzag width to 1.5. Use variegated blues and black thread on the black areas and variegated pale yellow thread on the belly area. Stitch in the direction of the feathers and sew on all the outer edges of all the pieces.

ADDITIONAL STITCHING

Press Blocks 5 and 6, treating them as one unit. Start in the center, press up, down, and to both sides.

For the steps in this section, use a straight stitch and solid-colored threads. For more details, see page 27.

Block 5

1. **Board and rope.** Use three brown threads. First, use a medium and dark brown thread, finishing with a light tan to highlight and create a "worn" wood appearance. Use medium brown thread to add detail and shading on the wood. Create the wood grain in the correct direction. Next, use the dark brown thread to shade and outline the whole post to define the edges. Lastly, use the tan thread to add more detail and highlighting. Do not forget all the little pieces of fencing behind the flowers!

2. **Pegs.** Use dark brown to outline and define the shape. This will also help separate the pegs from the board.

Remember!

I do not try to avoid or purposely sew on the variegated threads. I add these additional solid colored threads to blend and *add* to the thread work.

3. Leaves. Use multiple and different combinations of the numerous green threads. Similar to the same combinations of green threads used on Block 2 (see page 48) and Block 3 (see page 58). Layer the threads for additional shading and detail. It is important to follow the line patterns of detail for the different leaves.

5. Black-eyed Susans. Complete these flowers in the same stitching manner as the sunflowers, but with two threads and different color combinations. For the petals, use dark yellow and orange thread. Since the pieces are smaller, be mindful not to add too many threads. The centers are created with dark brown thread, outlining the edges and adding additional stitching for shade and texture.

4. Sunflowers. Follow the steps for the sunflowers on Block 4 (see page 70). I added slightly darker shades on these sunflowers to give them a more "aged" and "dry" appearance.

6. Gomphrena globe flower. Stitch these flowers in the same manner as the centers of the purple coneflowers in Block 3 (see page 59). Create the ombré appearance with three thread colors. The first layer is orange, which is then layered with bright orange, and finished with red on the top.

7. Lilacs. Use multiple layers of four purple threads to shade and blend a soft and natural appearance on the petals. Remember to connect the stitching, blending and slightly overlapping the previous threads.

Tip

Sew the layers in small and irregular stitches, overlapping the different threads and blending them together. Starting with the lighter lilac thread, shade from the top down to the bottom of each cluster. Layer to finish with the darker purple in the innermost center and bottom of each cluster.

8. Aster. Follow the steps for the asters on Block 4 (see page 71). I added slightly darker shades on these asters to give them a more "aged" and "dry" appearance.

9. Ribbons. Use a medium blue thread to add detail and shading on the ribbon. Create shading in the correct direction of the ribbons. Next, use the dark blue thread to outline the ribbon pieces to define the edges.

10. Tags. Use medium gray thread and only outline the edges.

11. Bird. First, use medium red thread, start from the tail and move to the head. Sew small stitches to imitate the layering of feathers. Next, add maroon thread to define, shade, and separate the chest, wings and neck areas. Then add dark maroon thread to add shaping and separation of the wing and tail. Follow this by adding black thread to the mask area on the face, blending the layers of stitching into the red areas. Finish by using dark orange to outline the beak.

12. Press. Even if you have been pressing the block throughout the above steps, iron the block again.

Tip

When working on the bird, it is best to start from the tail and work up the body to the head. Overlap the stitching, but also be mindful of the direction of the different body parts.

Block 6

1. Snow. Use a metallic iridescent thread to help create sparkle and shimmer on the snow. Sew along the outer edges and inside to add more color and to flatten the snow areas.

2. Leaves. Use multiple and different combinations of the numerous green threads for the flower leaves. They will be similar to the same combinations of green threads used on Block 2 (see page 48) and Block 3 (see page 58).

Layer the threads for additional shading and detail. It is important to follow the line patterns of detail for the different leaves. See Block 2 and Block 3 for possible thread combinations or create new ones.

3. Fall leaves. Use three thread colors, from orange to maroon. Layer them as the leaves in the previous step.

4. Snowdrops. Use three threads to create the shading on the bell caps and under areas. First, use white thread on the bottom edges of the white areas. Next, on the blue areas, layer medium and dark blue threads. Start the shading from the top of the bell, finishing with outlining only on the blue caps.

5. Crocus. Use three thread colors—medium purple, magenta, and purple—on the petals. Add yellow thread for the flower centers. To start shading the flowers and buds, use a slightly darker purple thread than the actual fabric. Use this thread to highlight and add shape to the petals. I like to see the fabric and variegated thread, as the additional colors help with the shading.

Next, use a maroon thread to blend all the colors together. Before adding the last thread on the petals, add yellow spikes in the center. Lastly, add dark purple thread to outline and define the individual petals.

6. Primroses. Use three shades of yellow threads—light yellow, mustard yellow, and metallic gold—for the petals and medium lime green for the centers. On each petal, sew along the edges and add some stitching coming from the inner areas on the petals (branching off from the center of each flower). This is similar to the stitching done on the purple coneflowers and zinnias on Block 3 (see page 59).

Use light yellow for shading along edges and tips of the petals, followed by mustard yellow to add more shading. Outline to define each petal. Next, add metallic gold to add highlighting and sparkle from the center of the petals.

Use medium lime green thread for the centers. Change the machine setting to a zigzag 1.5 width and 0.0 length and stitch, remaining in place for numerous stitches. This will create a buildup in the same area and form the appearance of a French knot.

7. Daffodils. These flowers are approached as two separate parts, the outer petals and the cup. Use three shades of yellow threads—yellow, mustard yellow, and dark mustard—on the outer petals. On each petal, sew along the edges and add some stitching coming from the inner areas (branching off from the center of each flower).

Layer the threads from the lightest to the darkest yellow, with the darkest colors primarily in the most center areas. Use the darkest yellow to outline and define each petal.

Use peach and orange threads for the cups. With the peach threads, shade from the inner areas (closest to the center) and move the shading toward the edges of the cup. With the orange thread, add shading to the under area of the cup and outline and define the shape of the cup.

8. Bird. As with birds on other blocks, it is best to start from the belly, working up the body and wings to the head. Overlap the stitching but also be mindful of the direction of the different body parts.

On the white belly area, use white thread. Start from the bottom of the belly and move to the neck. Sew small stitches to imitate the layering of feathers. Add light gray along the edge to create a separation between the bird and snow mound.

On the rest of the bird's body, start by adding light gray along the tail and wing areas. Overlap the stitches to blend the feathers together. Add medium gray thread to highlight the areas that need a separation of body parts and a pop of color. Use dark gray to define and separate the different body parts. Also, add some stitching to blend and create feathers.

With black thread, add an eye (use a small zigzag stitch, sewn in place). Add white thread along the tips of the wings and tail and dark mustard threads to shade and outline the beak.

9. Press. Even if you have been pressing the block throughout the previous steps, iron the block again.

Tip

The outer petals will have the darkest color near the center, but the cup will start with the lightest color near the center. For both flower parts, start with the lightest thread color and outline with the darkest colors.

10. Add grass spikes or curlicues. Look for any raised bumps or uneven treading or quilting. If there are any areas of concern, flatten the quilt with additional quilting, grass spikes, or curlicues! See step 11 on page 40 for more instruction.

CHAPTER 9

Outer Sashing and Border

Blocking and Squaring the Quilt

BLOCKING

All the free-motion quilting and thread painting is completed on all six blocks! Even though you have been ironing throughout the quilting and thread-painting processes, the quilt may still be misshapen and wrinkled. Since you have added more fabric and threads with each block, there's increased possibility for potential issues. Correct this by pressing the full quilt using following steps.

1. On a large open space, one that is slightly larger than the quilt, press the quilt with a very hot steam iron. (The area for pressing should be flat and able to get wet from the steam.)

On the back of the quilt, press from the center and side to side. Then iron from the center of the quilt to the top. Move the iron up and out to the sides. Repeat on the bottom of the quilt. Make sure the batting and muslin, where the outer border is going to be added, is flat and has no bumps or pleats.

2. Flip the quilt over to the front and repeat the previous step for ironing. Pay extra attention to the

Blocks 1 and 2 with blocking completed.

Tip

If your measurements haven't matched mine throughout the making of the quilt, just add a ½" (1.3cm) to the width (before sashing measurements), 1" (2.5cm) to the length, and ½" (1.3cm) on both ends of the length). Having the sashing slightly wider and longer will make it easier to sew on the outer border and maintain a straight line.

Make sure to check for straightness in multiple areas. Use as many reference points as you can find, using sashing pieces and design elements within the blocks.

design elements that need to be straight, such as the sashing pieces, fences, trellis, etc. Make sure they are as straight as possible. If misshapen, pull and tug on the fabric to correct the shape. Use a ruler to check the straightness of the lines. Place something heavy on the area, such as a few books or cans, to help keep the quilt straight while drying.

3. Let the quilt dry completely without moving it. This allows all the fibers and threads to shrink and bond together evenly prior to squaring the quilt.

SQUARING

Once the quilt is totally dry, it can be squared and prepared for adding the outer sashing and outer border.

1. Place largest ruler or rulers on the quilt and work off of as many horizontal and vertical lines on the quilt as possible (sashing pieces, trellis, fence post, flower stems, etc.) Use these reference lines to aide in squaring the quilt.

2. Mark the squaring lines and connect all lines on sides, top and bottom. Make sure that all batting will be covered when the sashing is added. Notice how distorted the quilt became from all the stitching.

3. From the marked lines, measure the width and length of the quilt in several places to check to make sure the measurements are all the same.

Adding the Outer Sashing

Your quilt now has all the blocks joined, blocked, and squared. It's time to add the outer sashing.

1. Measure from the marked squared placement lines, corner to corner on the *top* and *bottom*. They should measure approximately 40" (101.6cm). Cut two strips 2½" x 41" (6.4 x 104.1cm).

2. Place the top and bottom strips (right sides together) on the inside of the marked placement line. The sashing should have the extra ½" (1.3cm) on each end. Pin in place. Sew a ¼" (0.6cm) line to attach top and bottom sashing pieces.

3. Flip the top and bottom sashing pieces to the right side and press flat. Extend the side placement lines onto the sashing pieces at the top and bottom of the quilt.

4. Measure from the top edge of the top sashing to the bottom edge of the bottom sashing. This should measure approximately 38" (96.5cm). (Adjust to your quilt's measurements as needed.)

5. Cut two strips to 2½" x 39" (6.4 x 99.1cm) each for the sashing pieces.

6. Place the side sashing pieces (right sides together) on the inside of the placement line. Use a ¼" (0.6cm) seam allowance to attach the side sashing. Flip side sashings over to right side and press flat.

7. On all four sides, topstitch around the inner ⅛" (0.3cm) edge of the sashing pieces to secure in place.

8. Measure and mark a new 2" (5.1cm) square line on the two side sashing pieces. To secure the sashing to the batting and backing fabric, sew a basting stitch outside of the new placement line.

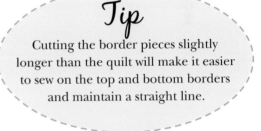

Tip

Cutting the border pieces slightly longer than the quilt will make it easier to sew on the top and bottom borders and maintain a straight line.

Adding and Quilting the Outer Border

ADDING THE OUTER BORDER
The outer border uses the same fabric as the block backgrounds.

1. Start by adding the side borders. Measure the side sashing pieces from top to bottom. It should be approximately 38" (96.5cm).

2. Cut two strips 5" x 39" (12.7 x 99.1cm) each (adjust to your measurements as needed). This will add ½" (1.3cm) to both ends of the strips so the pieces are 1" (2.5cm) longer than the quilt.

3. With right sides together, place the side border strips on the inside of the sashing placement line. The borders should have an extra ½" (1.3cm) on each end. Sew with a ¼" (0.6cm) seam allowance to attach the side borders.

4. Flip the side borders to the right side and press flat.

5. Extend the top and bottom placement lines onto the sewn side borders.

6. Measure from the outer edge of the left side border to the outer edge of the right side border. It should be approximately 52" (132.1cm).

7. Cut the two border strips 5" x 52" (12.7 x 132.1cm) each. (Notice that they will match the length of the quilt, plus the two side borders.)

8. With right sides together, place the top and bottom borders on the inside of the placement line. Sew with a ¼" (0.6cm) seam allowance to attach the top and bottom borders.

9. Flip the top and bottom borders over to right side and iron flat. Make sure the borders are lying flat on the batting.

10. Sew a ⅛" (0.3cm) topstitch line around the perimeter of the outer edge. This step helps to secure the sashing and maintain straight lines.

QUILTING THE OUTER BORDER

The outer borders are attached and now will need to be quilted prior to adding the appliqué pieces. When creating the blocks in previous chapters, the appliqué pieces were added before quilting. Create the border in reverse to help secure the long lines on the sashing.

1. Iron and press all three layers flat, starting closer to the sashing and moving to the outer edges.

2. Free motion quilt the background with a Topstitch 80/12 needle. Use the Poly Sheen thread that matches the background fabric in the top and bobbin. Working in small sections, start from the middle of each border and always move from the inner center to the outer edges.

3. When you are finished quilting to the edge in one section, cut the threads and start from the inner edge again and work your way out. Continue to free-motion quilt the outer border background until finished.

Your quilt should look similar to this once the outer border has been quilted.

Here is a closer look at the quilted border. Remember to always work in small sections and quilt from the inner center to the outer edges.

Designing the Outer Border

MATERIALS

+ Pattern, page 123
+ Freezer paper
+ Appliqué fabric suggestions: batiks and ombré cottons, in 3–4 medium greens and 2 medium browns
- Leaves: 3–4 medium greens (#1, #2, and #3); make approximately 110–120 total leaves from different green fabrics
- Twigs: 2 medium browns (#4, #5, and #6); make approximately 110 total branch pieces from different brown fabrics

THREADS

+ Variegated threads:
- Mettler Silk Finished Cotton 50 Multi
  - #9818 – mixed dark greens
  - #9817 – mixed lime greens
  - #9852 – mixed dark brown
- Poly Sheen Multi
  - 9932 – mixed green
+ Solid-colored threads:
- Mettler Silk Finished Cottons 50 Multi
  - #1425 – medium brown
  - #1002 – dark brown
  - #0092 – medium green
  - #224 – medium green
  - #0757 – dark green
  - #0314 – dark green
+ Metallic
- Mettler
  - #5833 – green

DESIGNING

Lay out the border as suggested. When placing the pieces along the sides, top, and bottom borders, take into consideration that you will soon be squaring and finishing the quilt. Be mindful not to place the pieces to close to the edge of the fabric. You do need open space on the outer edge where the binding will be added. Remember to balance the design and maintain the same spacing on each side. I suggest you randomly mark a guideline (such as 4" [10.2cm] from the sashing) along the border as a reminder to not have the pieces go past the line.

When happy with the placement and design, iron the appliqué pieces (with a pressing cloth placed over the pieces) in place to adhere to the background fabric.

> *Tip*
>
> These amounts are suggestions; you may use more or less than I did on your quilt. As long as you create an even and balanced look on all four sides of the border, the number of branches and leaves doesn't matter.

The appliqué border helps to frame the quilt and tie all the block designs together as one harmonious unit.

Stack the leaves over and under the branch pieces for a realistic look.

Thread Painting

BASE STITCHING

Set your machine to a zigzag stitch with a width of 2.0 and length of 0.0. Use a Topstitch 80 needle. For more information, see page 26.

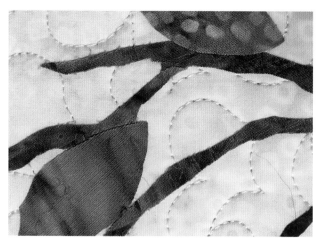

1. Branches. Use variegated brown thread. Sew along the outer edges of the twig parts, adding detailed stitching in the middle to create wood grain. Remember to sew in the correct direction of the twig parts.

2. Leaves. Use a variety of the variegated green thread on the different leaves. As in prior blocks, mix up the usage of the variegated greens, but use one variegated green thread on one specific leaf.

ADDITIONAL STITCHING

Iron the quilt from the middle of each border, pressing to the outer edges.

For the following steps, use a straight stitch and solid-colored threads. For more information, see page 27.

1. Branches. Use 2–3 thread colors. First, with a medium brown thread, add detail and shading to the wood. Create the wood grain in the correct direction. Next, use the dark brown thread to shade and outline all the posts to define the edges.

2. Leaves. Use multiple and different combinations of the numerous green threads. This will be similar to the same combinations of green threads used throughout the quilt. Layer the threads for additional shading and detail. It is important to follow the line patterns of detail for the different leaves. See prior blocks for possible thread combinations or create new ones.

3. **Press.** Even if you have been ironing the quilt throughout the previous steps, iron the quilt again.

4. **Add twigs or curlicues.** Look for any raised bumps or uneven threading or quilting. If there are any areas of concern, either do additional quilting or add the twigs from the branches or curlicues.

First, add the twigs and curlicues where needed, and then add others to balance the added stitching. If the border is perfectly flat, add the curlicues to soften the designs, lend a natural feel to the block, and balance the completed blocks' stitching.

CHAPTER 10

Finishing the Quilt

Before the backing is attached, you need to block the quilt . . . again! All the free-motion quilting and thread painting is completed on all six blocks and outer border, *except* for the quilting on the sashing pieces.

Blocking

Follow the same process for blocking your quilt as on page 89. Make sure the quilt is flat.

Adding Backing

1. Trim the extra batting and muslin to within 1"–2" (2.5–5.1cm) from the outer border. This will help to remove some of the bulk, as well as get a more accurate measurement for the backing.

2. Measure the size of the quilt, including the remaining batting and muslin.

3. Add 2" (5.1cm) to the width and length of the measurements from step 2. Use the previously cut extra-wide backing fabric and adjust the measurements as needed. Press the backing flat and remove all wrinkles.

4. Tape or pin the backing with the wrong side up to a floor or board. I find that using a foam board makes it possible to pin the backing in place, flat and taut.

5. Center the quilt on top of the backing. Pin the backing and quilt together starting from the center and working out to the outer edges. Pay attention to all of the sashing pieces and keep them as straight as possible.

Tip

Choose a quilt design that matches the overall design. I quilted an open leaf design that blended well with the background quilting.

It is very helpful to use large rulers while pinning to check to keep the lines as straight as possible.

Be sure to begin pinning in the center and work your way out to the edges to ensure no bubbles form in the quilt top or backing fabric.

Quilting and Finishing the Sashing

QUILTING THE SASHING

1. Free motion quilt the sashing areas. Use the same Poly Sheen thread previously used on the sashing pieces.

Start from the center of the sashing that stretches across the top of Blocks 1, 2, and 4. Gradually travel around the quilt, working up, down, and out to the outer sashing pieces. Cut the threads and restart if needed to get to a different area. Finish with the outer border.

2. Iron the quilt (again!) on a flat surface. Make sure everything still looks good and the lines are as straight as possible!

> *Tip*
> It may be very helpful to fold the quilt and use the bike clamps to reduce the bulk and weight of the quilt as you move it through your machine.

ADDING BLACK BIAS TAPE

If you are happy with the quilt without adding the black bias tape, you can skip this section and proceed to Squaring the Quilt (see page 98).

I added the black bias tape for two reasons: (1) I thought the bias tape framed each block and gave a visual pop to the blocks, and (2) it is a wonderful aide to correct the squaring of each block. If the blocks become wonky and not square, this straight, linear trim will correct this.

1. With the largest ruler or rulers, re-square Block 1 first, working off the sashing lines. Look at the vertical and horizontal lines from the sashing pieces (as many as possible). For instance, check on all four sides of Block 1 and, if possible, any other sashing lines.

2. At this point, you may notice that the block is not as straight as it first appeared. That is okay! When you mark the lines for where the tape will be added, make sure you do not see either the sashing or the background fabric on either side of where the tape will be added.

3. Remove the paper from the bias tape and place it on the marked lines. Press in place. Make sure the lines remain straight! At the corners, fold the tape and miter them to create a nice point.

4. Using black thread and a straight stitch, sew as close to the edge of the tape as possible. Repeat on the other side of the tape.

5. Repeat the same process of marking on the remaining blocks:

Use Block 1's bias tape and other sashing lines to mark Block 2's bias tape placement. Block 2 only needs three lines: top, left side, and bottom.

Using bias tape is a great way to hide mistakes. For example, when applied, you do not see the sashing fabric where there should be the background fabric.

> *Tip*
> As well as you can, be mindful to keep all of the sashing pieces the same width once you add the bias tape. There should be approximately 1½" (3.8cm) across the width of each sashing from one bias tape to another.

Use the bias tape around Block 1 and Block 2 to mark Block 3's bias tape placement. Block 3 only needs two lines: top and left side.

Use the bias tape around Block 1 and Block 3 to mark Block 4's bias tape placement. Block 4 only needs two lines: top and right side.

Use the bias tape around Blocks 4, 1, and 2 to mark the bias tape placement for Block 5 and Block 6. Block 5 only needs two lines: bottom and right side; Block 6 only needs 2 lines, bottom and left side.

6. Mark the inner bias tape placement lines of the outer sashing. Use the bias tape lines on all the completed blocks to mark the inner sashing lines. Repeat with the other side of the outer sashing lines.

Squaring the Quilt and Adding the Binding

1. After completing the sashing and bias tape, you need to iron the quilt again! Repeat the same process as previously instructed on page 90. Remember to let the quilt dry completely before moving on.

2. If you see areas of bumps on the quilt or it is not lying flat, go back into the quilt and add some free-motion quilting, curlicues, or outline a few leaves or flowers. Be careful not to add too much quilting! You have squared up with the quilt with bias tape lines and do not want to pull in those lines with too much additional quilting.

3. Lay the quilt on a large flat area and iron it flat again. Use a large ruler (8" x 24" [20 x 61cm] or similar) to mark the outer border. Use the bias tape lines as you quilt. Mark all four sides to square the quilt. I went 4" (10.2cm) off the outer bias tape line. After marking, measure the quilt for even measurements in multiple areas, vertically and horizontally.

4. When everything looks even, trim the excess batting and backing from the quilt on the marked lines.

5. Attach the binding as desired. I use a 2½" (6.4cm) binding sewn from the front and hand-sewn on the back.

Adding the Crystals

I love to add little crystals to my quilts because when the sun hits them, the sparkle draws you into the quilt. Just placing a few crystals here and there can change the effect of the whole quilt. Be mindful not to add too many crystals on the quilt. You don't want it to look too tacky. Remember, less is best!

Tip

Be careful when purchasing the crystals. If the crystals are labeled as "hot fixed," make sure the glue is fabric safe!

HOT-FIXED CRYSTALS

1. When applying hot-fixed crystals to the quilt, work in approximately 6" (15.2cm) square sections.

2. Place your crystals where desired, then carefully lay a pressing cloth over them.

3. Use a small iron on the pressing cloth and press for about 10 seconds. Reapply the heat if the glue hasn't fully melted.

If the crystals are not hot fixed, attach them to the quilt with E6000 glue.

Take notice that I only placed the crystals on the fall leaves, holly, and grass spikes. Use them sparingly to give the piece interest that doesn't overwhelm.

Congratulations!
Great job and enjoy your beautiful quilt!

Block 5

Block 6

Block 4

Block 1

Block 2

Block 3

Patterns

BLOCK 1 *See page 30.*

✢ Watering can:
   - Medium gray – #1, 3
   - Dark gray – #2, 4–7
✢ Shovel:
   - Medium gray – #8
   - Medium blue – #9
✢ Trowel:
   - Medium gray – #10
   - Medium blue – #11
✢ Gloves:
   - Tan – #12, 13
   - Blue – #14, 15
✢ Basket:
   - Brown – #16
   - Dark brown – #17, 18
✢ Bird:
   - Yellow – #19
   - Black – #20–23
✢ Lavender:
   (make 14–16 flowers, 6 stems, and
   6–8 leaves)
   - Variety of purples – #24–29
   - Variety of greens – #30–35
✢ Clematis:
   (7–8 flowers, 15–16 buds, and
   80–85 leaves)
   - Green (leaves) – #36–38
   - Pink (buds) – #40–42
   - Pink (petals) – #43–56
   - Yellow (centers) – #57, 58
✢ Trellis:
   - Ivory/tan – #59–69
    (#64–68 reverse design)

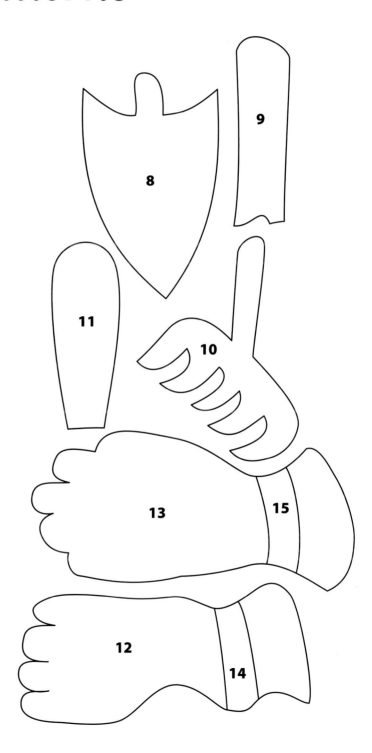

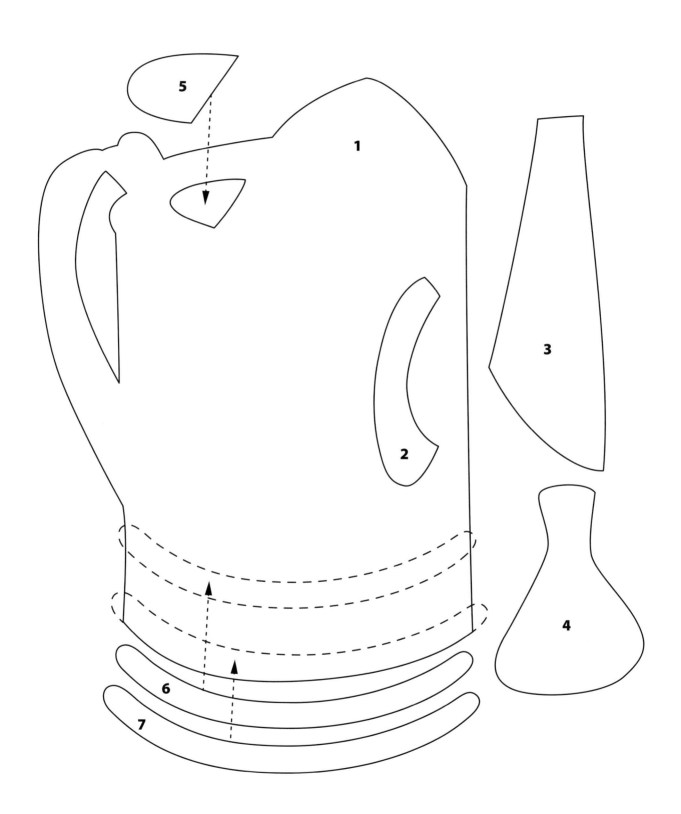

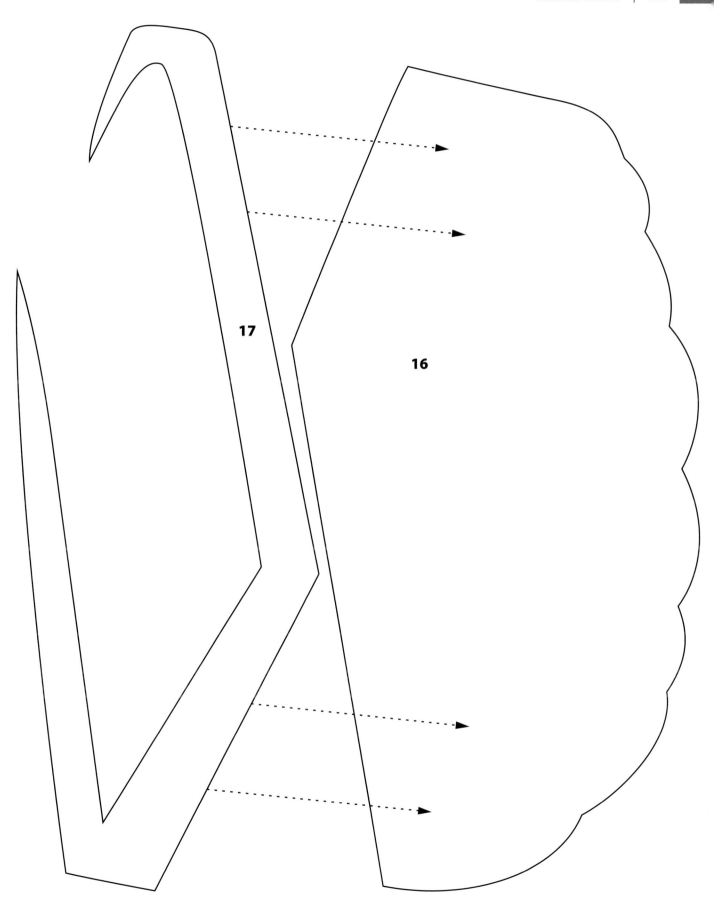

17

16

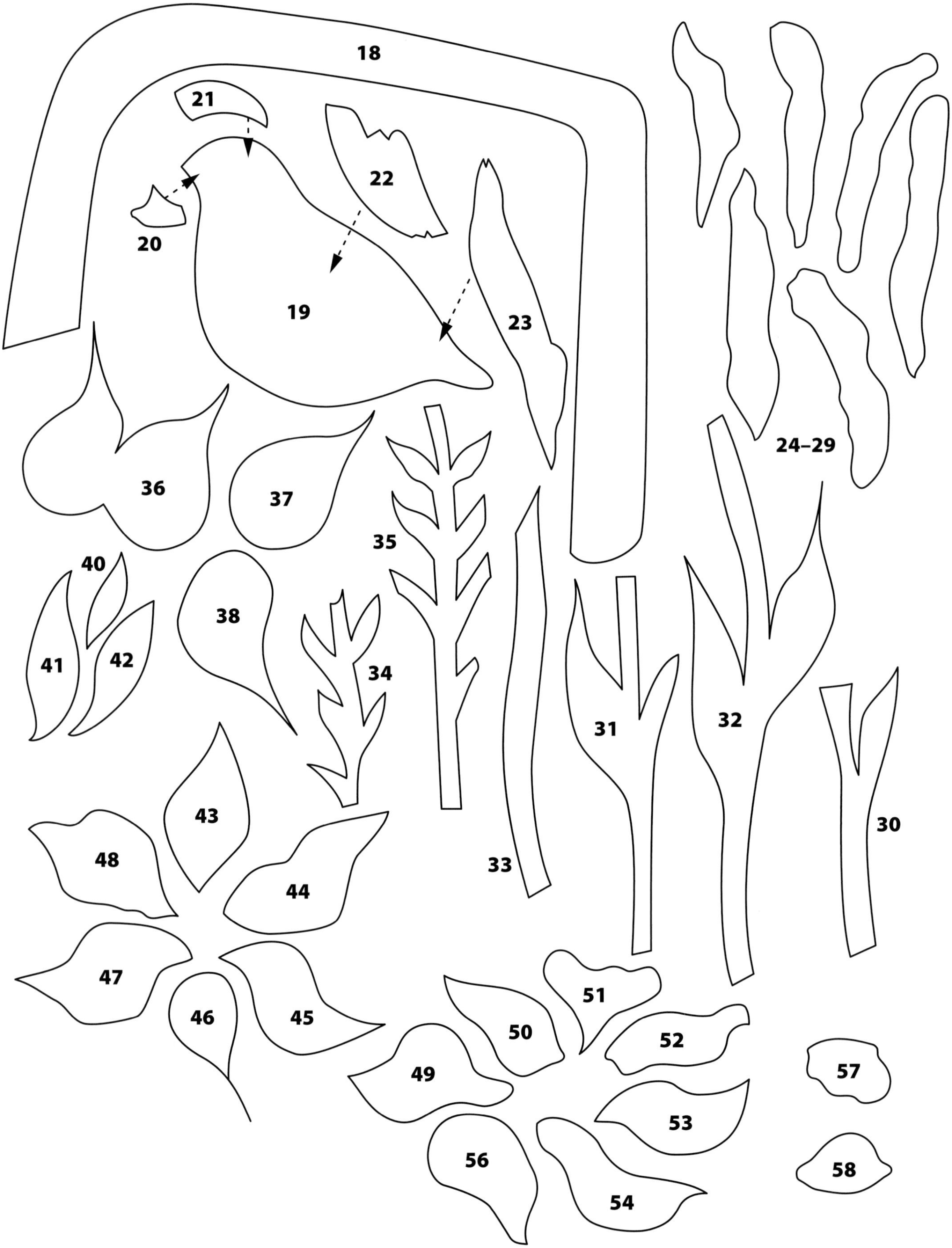

18

21

22

20

19

23

24–29

36

37

35

40

38

34

41

42

31

32

30

33

43

48

44

47

46

45

51

50

52

57

49

53

56

54

58

59

60

61

62

63

68

69

*64
R

*65
R

*66
R

*67
R

*64–67 Reverse Design

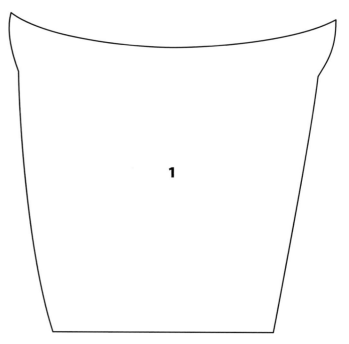

BLOCK 2 *See page 42.*

✢ Pots:
  - Light brown/rust – #1, 2
✢ Violets:
  - Mixed greens (leaves) – #3–5
    (make 8)
  - Mixed purples (flowers, buds) –
    #6, 7 *(make 6)*
✢ Lily of the valleys:
  - Medium green (leaves) –
    #10–13
  - Dark green (stems) – #14, 15
    (make 2)
  - White (flowers) – #16–18
    (make 16)
✢ Grass spike fillers:
  - Mixed dark greens – #19–21
    (make 8)
✢ Irises and bud:
  - Dark green – #22–25
  - Yellow – #27–31
  - Purple – #26, 32–34
  - Gold – #35, 36
✢ Magnolia flower, buds, and bark:
  - Dark brown – #37–39
  - Mixed pinks – #40–42 *(make 4)*
  - Mixed pinks – #43–47 *(make 1)*
✢ Lily and bud:
  - White – #48–51
  - Green (stem) – #52
  - White (flower) – #53–58
  - Yellow/pink (flower)
    – #53A–58A
  - Mixed greens (leaves) – #59, 60
    (make 6)
✢ Butterfly:
  - Black (body, wings) – #61–63
  - Blue (wings) – #64–65

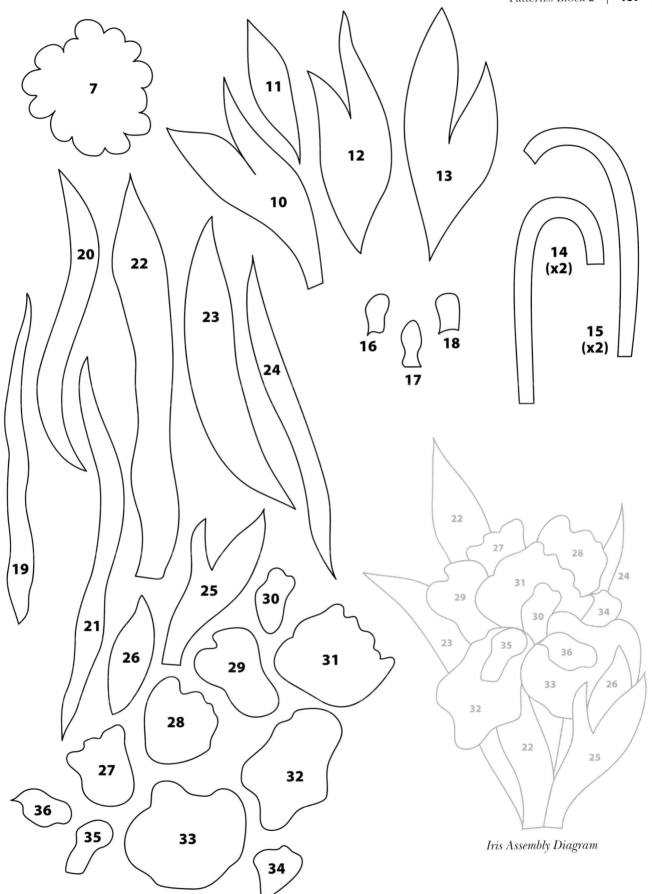

Iris Assembly Diagram

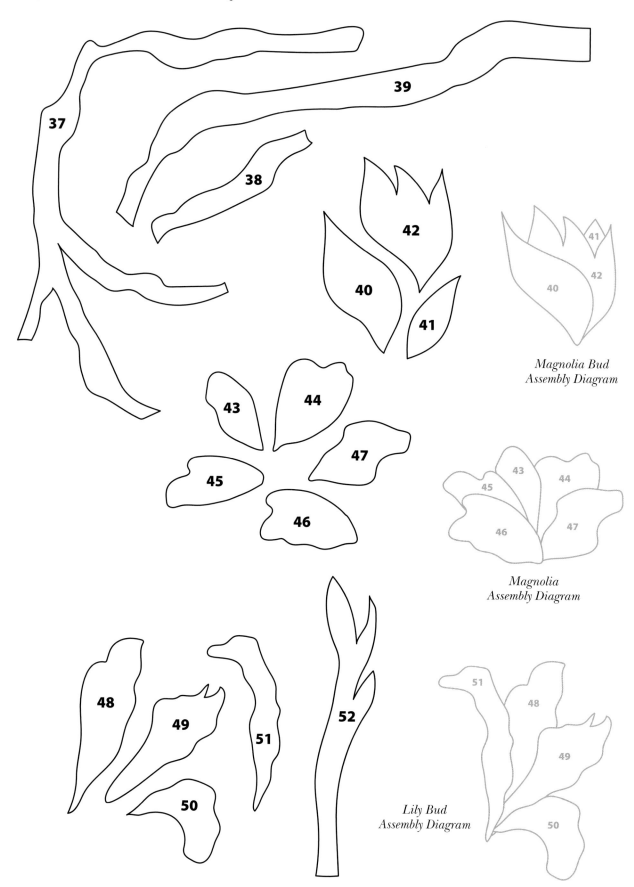

Magnolia Bud Assembly Diagram

Magnolia Assembly Diagram

Lily Bud Assembly Diagram

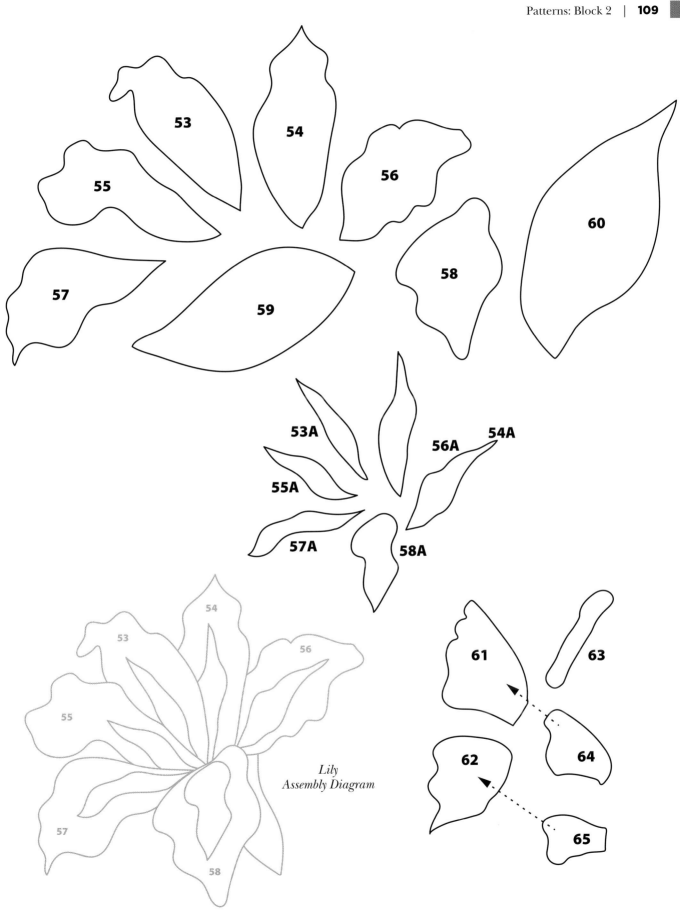

53

54

55

56

57

59

58

60

53A

55A

57A

54A

56A

58A

*Lily
Assembly Diagram*

54

53

56

55

57

58

61

63

62

64

65

BLOCK 3 *See page 53.*

✛ Fence:
- Tan (rails) – #1 *(make 9)*
- Tan (long board) – 1½" x 26"
  (3.8 x 66.04cm)

✛ Bird:
- Medium brown – #2
- Medium blue – #3, 5
- Rust – #4

✛ Butterflies:
- Yellow – #6, 7, 11–14
- Blue – #8, 9, 15–18
- Black – #10, 19

✛ Coneflowers:
- Purple (petals) – #20, 21
- Yellow (centers) – #22, 23
- Green (leaves) – #24–26
  (make 5–8)

✛ Ivy:
(make 5 of each shape)
- Mixed greens – #27–30
*(make 5 of each petal shape and
12–14 leaves)*
- Light blue – #31–36
- Medium blue – #37–42
- Dark blue – #43–48
- Green (leaves) – #49–51

✛ Zinnias:
- Dark orange/dark pink – #52
  (make 1 in each color)
- Medium/light orange/dark
  pink/purple – #53, 55 *(make 1 in
  each color)*
- Purple – #54
- Green – #56–58
- Light/dark pink – #59 *(make 2 in
  each color)*
- Purple/yellow – #60 *(make 2 in
  each color)*
- Dark orange – #61 *(make 3)*
- Light orange – #62 *(make 3)*
- Yellow – #63 *(make 3)*
- Mixed greens – #64–66

*Bird
Assembly Diagram*

*Butterfly
Assembly Diagram*

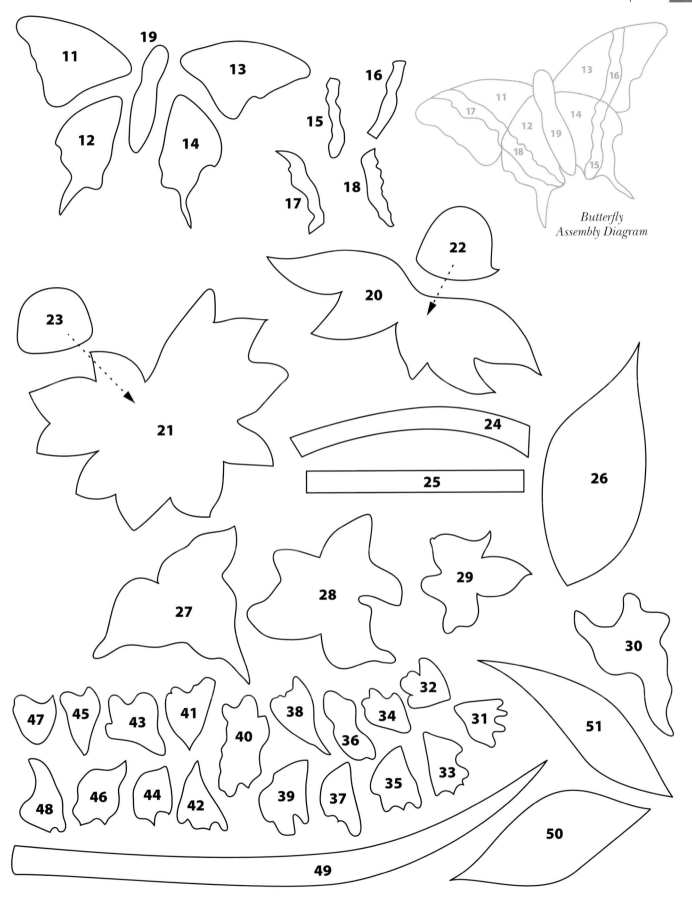

Butterfly
Assembly Diagram

Zinnia
Assembly Diagram

Zinnia
Assembly Diagram

BLOCK 4 *See page 62.*

✢ Post:
- Tan – 2" x 14¾"
  (5.1 x 37.47cm)

✢ House:
- Tan – #2, 3
- Dark blue – #4
- Medium blue – #5
- Medium brown – #6, 8
- Dark brown – #7

✢ Sunflowers:
(make 2 flowers, 1 bud, 1 of each bud leaf, and 8 large leaves)
- Mixed yellows – #9–21, #23–32
- Medium brown – #22
- Green – #33–37
- Mixed greens – #38–41

✢ Cosmos:
- Mixed pinks – #42–56
  (make 2 of each shape)
- Yellow – #57, 58
  (make 2 of each shape)
- Greens – #59–61
  (make 4 of each shape)

✢ Buddleias:
- Mixed purples – 62–66 *(make 2–3 of each shape)*
- Dark green – #67–69
  (make 5 of each shape)

✢ Gaillardias:
- Yellow – #70–75
  (make 3 of each shape)
- Rust/red – #70A–75A
  (make 3 of each shape)
- Maroon – #76 *(make 3)*
- Yellow – #77–80
- Rust/red – #77A–80A
- Green – #81–84

✢ Asters:
- Mixed purples – #85 *(make 3)*, 86
  (make 6), 87 *(make 1)*
- Yellow – #88 *(make 9)*
- Green – #89 *(make 1)*, 90 *(make 8)*

✢ Small Daisies:
- Yellow – #91 *(make 8)*
- Orange – #92 *(make 8)*
- Green – #93 *(make 12)*

✢ Berries and borders:
(make enough to fill areas)
- Browns – #94, 95
- Red – #96
- Green – #97

✢ Bird:
- Gray – #98, 100, 101
- Pale yellow – #99
- White – #102
- Brown – #103

✢ Butterfly:
- Black – #104–108
- Blue – #104A–107A

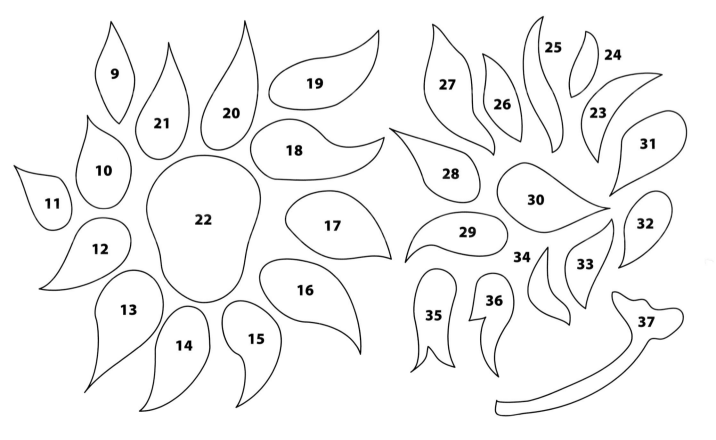

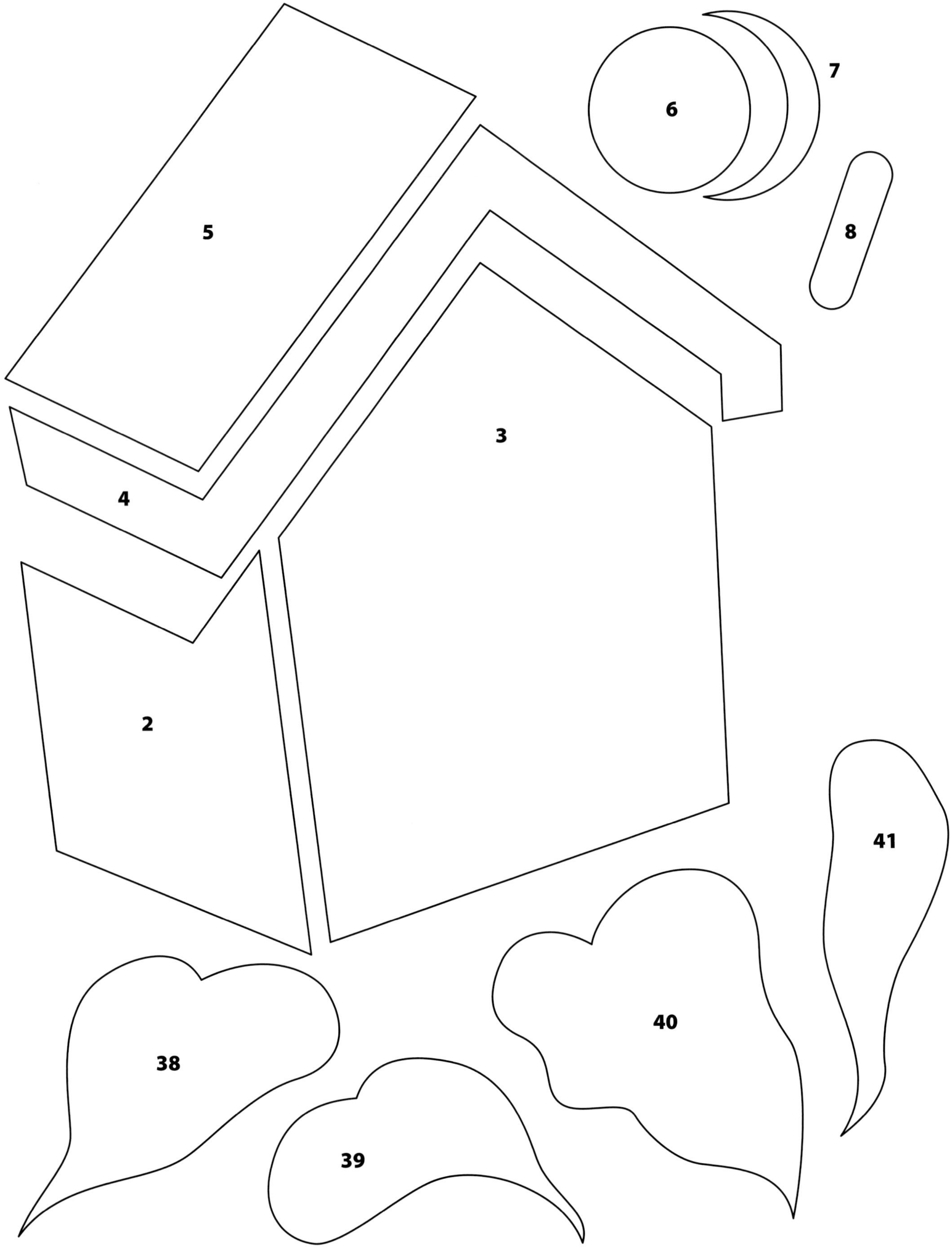

5

6

7

8

3

4

2

41

40

38

39

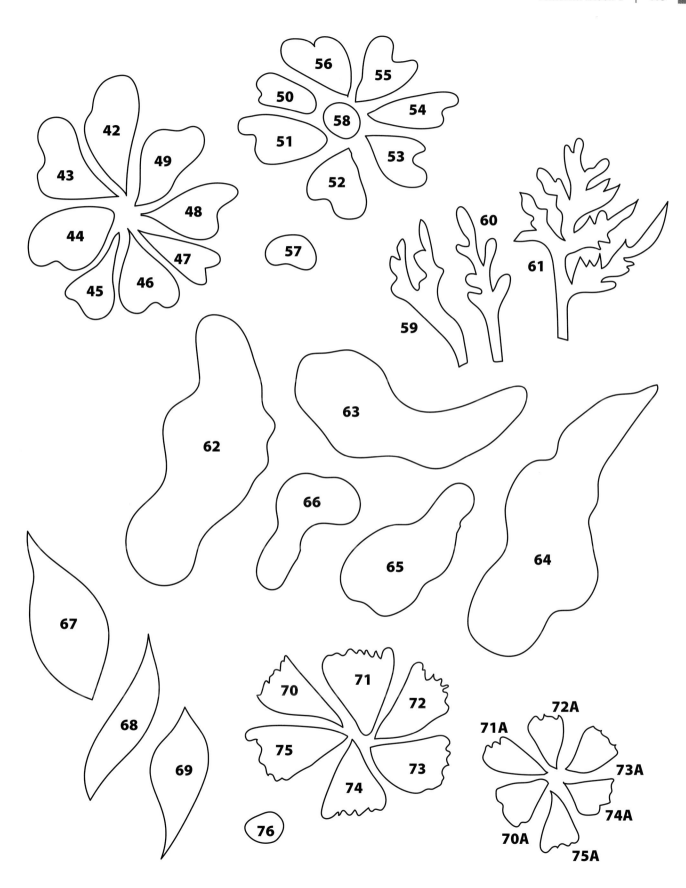

Bird Assembly Diagram

BLOCK 5 *See page 74.*

✢ Board:
  - Light brown – 1¾" x 18½" (4.45 x 47cm)
✢ Strings:
  - Light brown – ¼" x 6¾" (2 x 17.15cm) *(make 2)*
✢ Pegs:
  - Medium brown – #1
✢ Mini black-eyed Susans: *(make approx. 12–14 leaves, 5–6 stems, and 14–15 flowers)*
  - Mixed greens – #2–6 *(make 12 of each shape)*
  - Blue – #7–9
  - Yellow – #10
  - Brown – #11
  - Ivory – #12
✢ Lilacs:
  - Mixed greens – #13–14 *(make 3–5 of each shape)*
  - Mixed greens – #15 *(make 10)*
  - Mixed purples – #16–18 *(make 5 of each shape)*
  - Ivory – #19
  - Blue – #20–22
✢ Sunflowers:
  - Mixed greens – #23 *(make 3)*, 24 *(make 2)*
  - Ivory – #25
  - Blue – #26–28
  - Mixed yellows – #29–41 *(make 2 of each shape)*
  - Brown – #42 *(make 2)*
✢ Gomphrena globe flowers:
  - Mixed greens – #43, 44 *(make 10)*, 45 *(make 13)*
  - Mixed oranges – #46 *(make 14–15 flowers)*
  - Ivory – #47
  - Blue – #48–50
✢ Asters:
  - Mixed greens – #51–55 *(make 10–12)*
  - Ivory – #56
  - Blue – #57–59
  - Purple – #60 *(make 14)*
  - Yellow – #61 *(make 14)*
  - Green – #62 *(make 3)*
  - Purple – #63 *(make 3)*
✢ Holly:
  - Green – #64 *(make 3)*
✢ Cardinal:
  - Red – #65, 66
  - Black – #67
  - Dark orange – #68

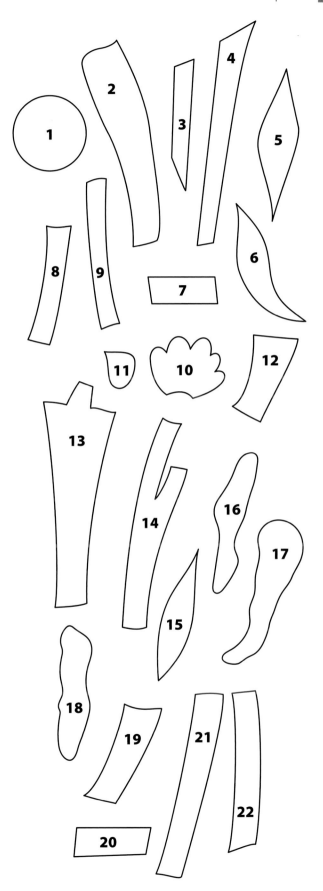

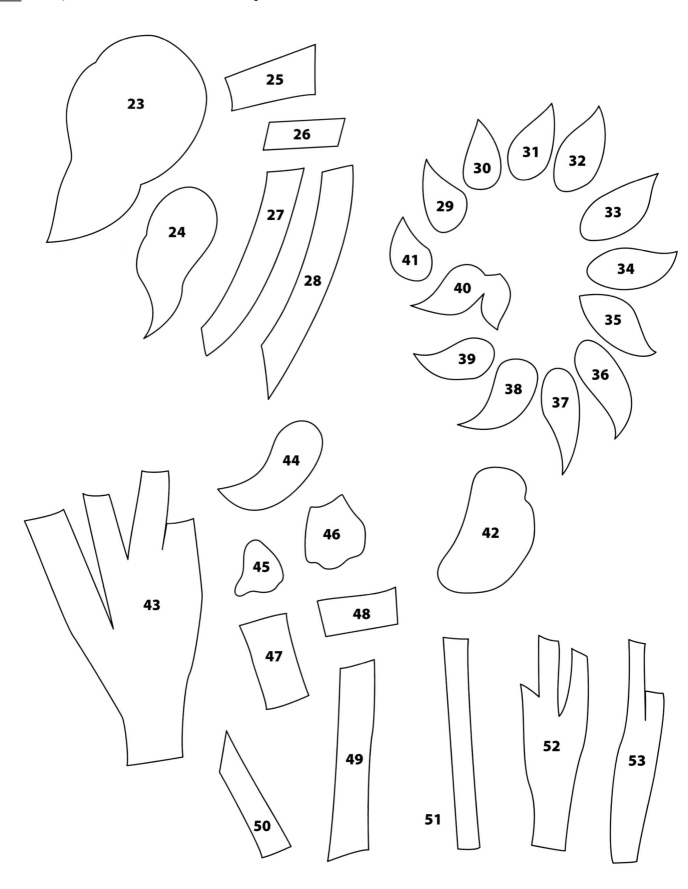

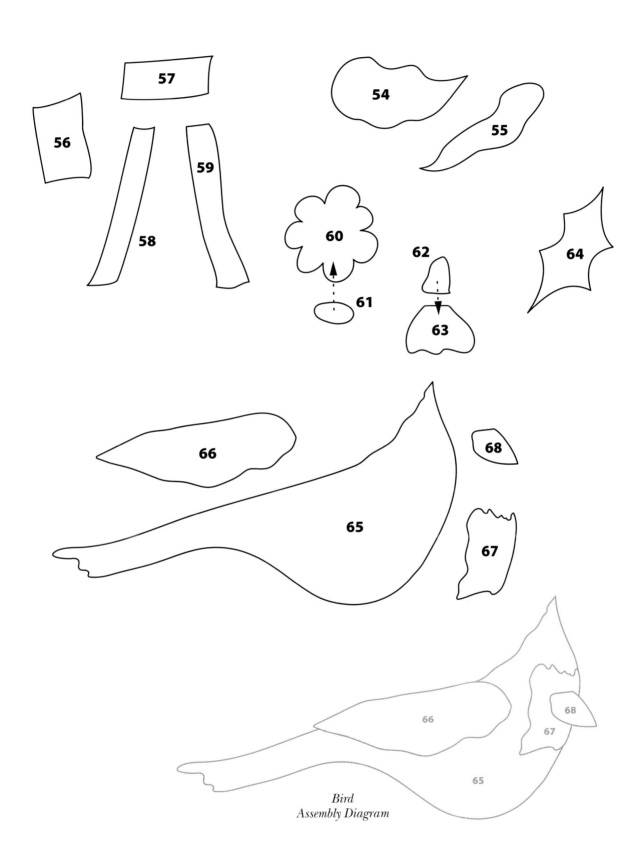

*Bird
Assembly Diagram*

BLOCK 6 *See page 74.*

✣ Fall oak leaves:
   - Orange/brown – #1–3 *(make 2 of each shape)*
✣ Holly:
   - Green – #4 *(make 4)*
✣ Snow mounds:
   - White – #5, 6 *(make 2 of each shape)*
✣ Primroses and buds:
   - Yellow – #7 *(make 4)*, 8 *(make 2)*
   - Brown – #9
   - Green – #10 *(make 5)*
✣ Crocuses:
   - Dark purple – #11 *(make 4)*
   - Yellow – #12 *(make 4)*
   - Medium purple – #13 *(make 4)*
   - Green – #14–16 *(make 2 of each shape)*
✣ Bird:
   - Dark gray – #17–18
   - White – #19
   - Yellow – #20
✣ Daffodils:
   - Green – #21–26
   - Yellow – #27, 28 *(make 2 of each shape)*
   - Light orange – #29 *(make 2)*
   - Orange – #30 *(make 2)*
   - Yellow – #31
   - Light orange – #32
   - Orange – #33
✣ Snowdrops:
   - Green – #34–41 *(make 2–3)*
   - Blue – #42, 43 *(make 7 of each shape)*
   - White – #44, 45 *(make 7 of each shape)*

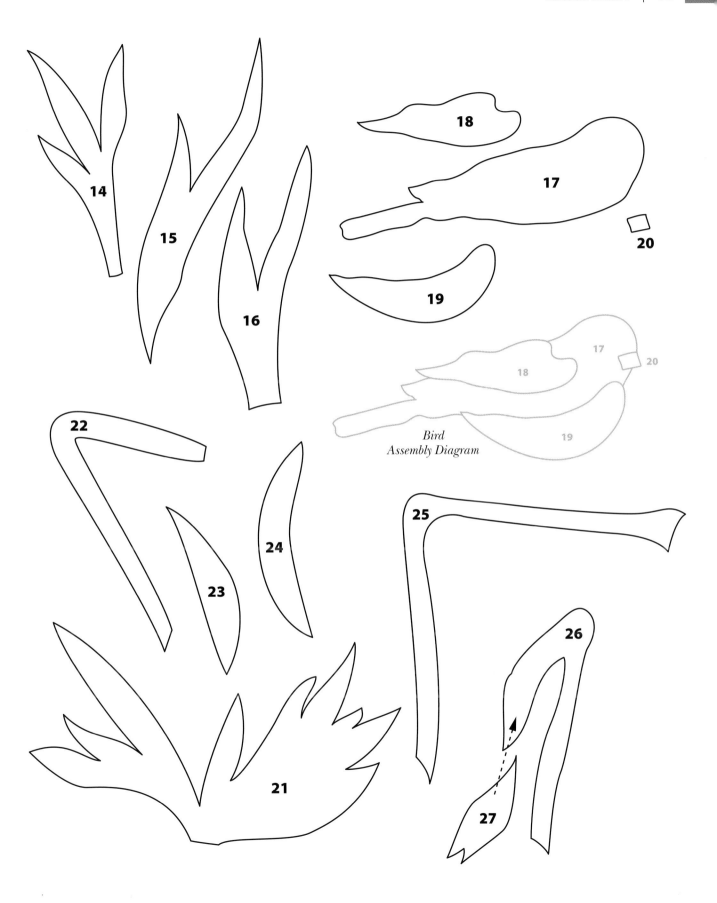

*Bird
Assembly Diagram*

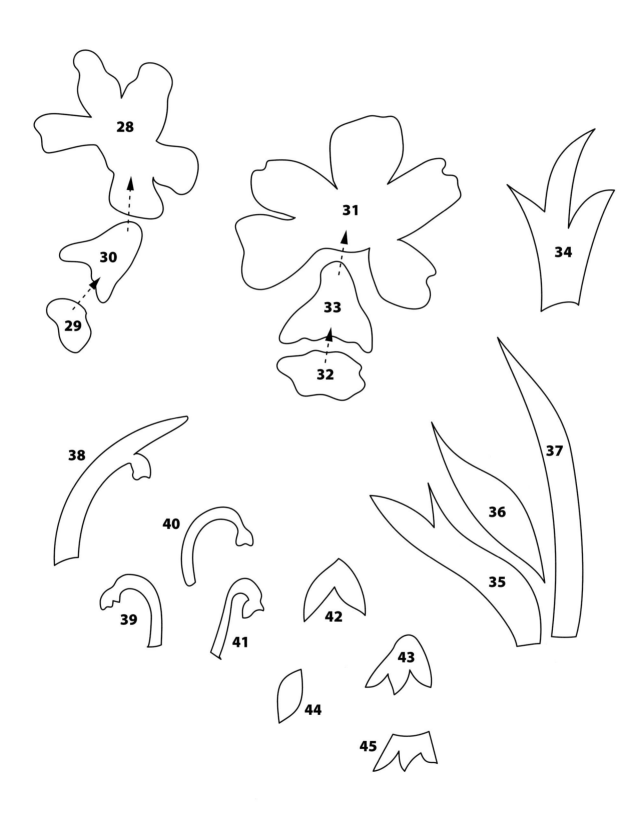

BORDER *See page 93.*

✤ Leaves:
- Mixed greens – #1–3 *(make 110–120)*

✤ Twigs:
- Mixed browns – #4–6 *(make 110)*

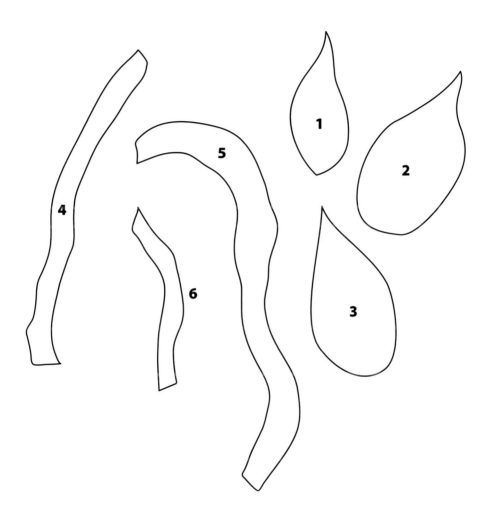

Resources

METTLER
Threads
www.Amann-Mettler.com

BROTHER™
Sewing machine and ScanNCut
www.Brother-USA.com

CUTTERPILLAR
Tracing board
www.CutterPillar.com

HOTFIX ADHESIVE™
Fusible adhesive
www.HotfixFabric.com

MOUNTAIN MIST CRAFTS
Wool mat
www.MountainMistCrafts.com

OLISO®
Irons
www.Oliso.com

SCHMETZ NEEDLES
Needles
www.SchmetzNeedles.com

THE WARM COMPANY
Batting and Lite Steam-A-Seam 2®
www.WarmCompany.com